TELEPHONE SURVEY METHODS

Sampling, Selection, and Supervision

Paul J. Lavrakas

Applied Social Research Methods Series
Volume 7

SAGE PUBLICATIONS
The International Professional Publishers
Newbury Park   London   New Delhi

APPLIED SOCIAL RESEARCH METHODS SERIES

Series Editor:
LEONARD BICKMAN, Peabody College, Vanderbilt University, Nashville
Series Associate Editor:
DEBRA J. ROG, Vanderbilt University, Washington, DC

TELEPHONE SURVEY METHODS

Sampling, Selection, and Supervision

Applied Social Research Methods Series
Volume 7

For information address:

SAGE Publications, Inc.
2111 West Hillcrest Drive
Newbury Park, California 91320

SAGE Publications Ltd.
28 Banner Street
London EC1Y 8QE
England

SAGE Publications India Pvt. Ltd.
M-32 Market
Greater Kailash I
New Delhi 110 048 India

Printed in the United States of America

Library of Congress Cataloging-in-Publication Data

Lavrakas, Paul J.
    Telephone survey methods.

    (Applied social research methods series ; v. 7)
    Bibliography: p.
    Includes index.
    1. Telephone surveys.   2. Social sciences—Research.
I. Title.   II. Series.
H91.L38   1986   300'.723   86-13079
ISBN 0-8039-2634-0
ISBN 0-8039-2635-9 (pbk.)

FIFTH PRINTING, 1990

CONTENTS

PREFACE

When asked to consider contributing a book to Sage's Applied Social Research Methods Series, I welcomed the opportunity to write a "how-to" text on telephone survey methods. Although several other fine texts address survey research in general and telephone surveying in particular, none takes the *applied* approach presented here. This text is filled with seemingly mundane yet very important details about a highly routinized process for gathering data via telephone surveys. Focusing on the mundane and specific when planning and implementing a telephone survey is necessary if quality data are to result.

As elaborated in this text, a primary advantage of telephone surveys over in-person and mail surveys is the opportunity they afford for instituting control over the quality of the entire survey process. Many persons who conduct telephone surveys appear not to recognize the importance of instituting a level of control that is most likely to assure the valid sampling and standardized interviewing that should be the goal of all quality telephone surveys. Or if they do recognize its importance, many seem unwilling to make the effort this requires.

Given the length of this text, it was impossible to address all aspects of the telephone survey process. Instead I chose three parts—sampling, selection, and supervision—that are not covered elsewhere in as much depth. In particular the science, art, and craft of developing quality questionnaires for use in telephone surveys are not addressed in this text. Rather, I address how to institute quality control over interviewers' use of questionnaires. Developing a quality questionnaire will not assure a surveyor of quality data unless quality sampling and quality interviewing also occur.

I have assumed that most users of this text are most likely to want to plan and implement local area telephone surveys, not regional or national ones. As such, many of the techniques for generating and processing telephone survey sampling pools discussed in this text concentrate on the local level. No one should attempt a regional or national telephone survey without experience with local ones.

This text does not explain the use of computer-assisted telephone interviewing (CATI). Although CATI will be available to more and more surveyors over the next decade, it is a new and still developing technology that I believe should be used by surveyors only *after* they have adequate experience conducting telephone surveys via the traditional paper-and-pencil techniques explained in this text.

I would like to thank Leonard Bickman and Debra Rog for the opportunity to write this text and the editorial assistance they and their reviewers provided. I wrote and revised the manuscript using WordStar on an IBM-PC. I thank Katie Roebuck for the help she provided in gathering information and in typing portions of the original manuscript and Jim Hansen for his proofreading. I also thank Susan F. Bennett and Susan M. Rosenbaum, two valued colleagues, whose abilities to manage research projects have allowed me to devote the attention needed to produce this text. Finally, I remain grateful to my wife, Barbara J. Lavrakas, and our son, Nikolas J. Lavrakas, for their continued support and the understanding they show toward the time I devote to my professional interests.

This text is dedicated to Len Bickman, Bob Boruch, Marilyn Brewer, Margo Gordon, Emil Posavac, Frank Slaymaker, and Wes Skogan. I remember and appreciate the intellectual stimulation and practical opportunities each has provided me, thereby helping to advance my interests in and experiences with applied research methods. It is also dedicated to Bob LeBailly, Jutta Sebestik, and Ron Szoc for all their technical help that directly and indirectly led to this text.

1

INTRODUCTION

Prior to the 1960s, the proportion of households in the United States with telephones was too low to justify the use of the telephone as a sampling medium. As such, "telephone survey methods" are a relatively new and still developing science and craft. The primary advantage afforded by properly structured telephone surveys over other in-person and mail surveys is the opportunity to monitor and control closely the quality of data collection as it occurs. Currently there are no social or physical barriers that automatically rule out consideration of telephone surveys, and in many instances they are the most cost-effective approach to gathering quality survey data.

Humans have a long history of being interested in quantification, the process of representing something in some measurable (numerical) form. Quantities hold intrinsic value beyond their mere symbolic representations of amount. Although in earlier periods there was less need for the average person to have a broad understanding of quantity, that need now pervades our lives. Even persons who consider themselves nonquantitative cannot deny the myriad decisions they make daily based on considerations of quantity.

Since historical times it has come to be recognized that an exact count or measure is not always needed for effective decision making. This recognition has served as the basis for the development of sampling theory. Sampling, or the process of taking into account *only a subset* of all possible elements of a larger set or population of persons, places, things, and so on, has long been implicit in human judgment. (This serves as the underpinnings of stereotyping, for example.) Much more recent, however, has been the development of formal methods to engage in *systematic* sampling, which brings us to those techniques thought of as "survey methods."

Survey methods are a collection of techniques for which the most typical purpose is to provide precise estimates of the prevalence (i.e., amount) of some variable of interest: for example, what percentage of registered voters are likely to vote for a certain candidate; what percentage of households own videocassette recorders; on what percentage of tests does a teacher make scoring errors; and what percentage of automobiles come off the assembly line with structural defects. In these examples one does not need an exhaustive measure of all possible voters, households, tests, or automobiles to gain information on which to base an accurate judgment about who will win the election, the size of the market for videotapes, the attention the teacher gives to grading, or the quality of workmanship at a particular assembly plant.

When survey methods are properly employed, the resulting estimates can be extremely precise representations of whatever is being measured. So precise are they that their "margin of error" is negligible, at least from the standpoint of effective decision making. Yet valid survey methods (i.e., those likely to be accurate) constitute a relatively new body of knowledge, which may explain why they are often misused.

TELEPHONE SURVEYS IN PERSPECTIVE

In particular, telephone survey methods have undergone serious development only in the last 20 years. Prior to that time the proportion of households in the United States with telephones was too low to justify the use of the telephone as a valid sampling medium. Once the proportion of U.S. households with telephones exceeded 90%, which occurred in the 1970s, it became theoretically possible to sample almost as comprehensively as with personal (face-to-face) interviewing. Telephone survey methods, however, are clearly based on the methodologies that developed in the last 60 years with face-to-face surveying.

By the mid-1980s telephone surveying had become commonplace, and in many instances it is the most preferred approach to surveying. It is a methodology that has achieved a respected status as a valid means of gathering information to aid effective decision making in both the public and private sectors. In fact, much more money is spent on telephone surveys by market researchers than by public opinion pollsters and academic researchers combined.

Figure 1 illustrates why telephone surveying has gained the prominence it merits as a means of providing precise estimates on some topic of interest. Simply stated, in most instances its advantages far outweigh its disadvantages. Although many fail to recognize or acknowledge it, by far the most important advantage of telephone surveying is the opportunity it provides for *quality control* over the entire data collection process. This includes sampling, respondent selection, and

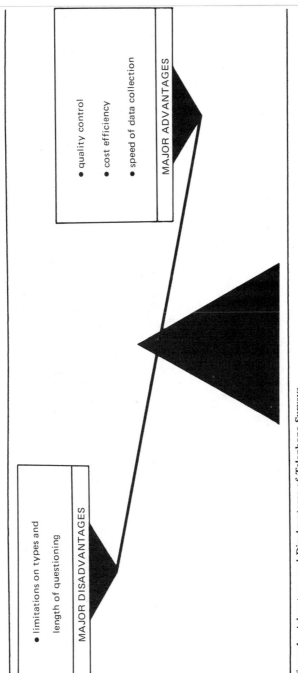

Figure 1. Advantages and Disadvantages of Telephone Surveys

the asking of questionnaire items. It is this advantage that almost always recommends the telephone as the preferred approach to surveying, providing there is no other overriding reason that rules against its use.

This text stresses the importance of controlling and monitoring the data collection process to ensure the gathering of high-quality data that can be used to provide precise estimates. No other approach to surveying provides this control over quality. When properly organized, interviewing done by telephoning most closely approaches the level of unbiased standardization that is the goal of all good surveys.

The second big advantage to telephone surveying is its cost-efficiency. Telephone surveys can collect data far more efficiently, from a cost standpoint, than in-person interviewing. Although they are typically more expensive than survey data collected by mail, their other advantages outweigh this disadvantage, except in those instances in which the available resources for funding data collection are so few as to rule out even use of the telephone.

The third major advantage of telephone surveying is the speed at which data can be gathered and thus processed. In a week or less one can gather data via telephone that might take a month or more using in-person interviews. An even longer period could be anticipated using a mail survey with follow-up mailings to increase typically low response rates. For example, with as few as ten experienced telephone interviewers working four-hour shifts, upwards of 400 to 500 20-item questionnaires could be easily completed within three days (including allowances for call-backs). If, for example, on Monday a mayor needed some information by the end of the week to aid an important policy decision (e.g., how dissatisfied are citizens with police services, and should she fire the police commissioner?), a good survey organization would be able to complete a telephone survey of adult residents and provide results to the mayor by the deadline.

The major disadvantage of telephone surveying, even when well executed, is its limitations on the complexity and length of the interview. Unlike the dynamics of face-to-face interviewing, it is tiresome to keep the average person on the telephone for longer than 20 or 30 minutes. In contrast personal interviewers do not seem to notice respondent fatigue, even with interviews that last 30-40 minutes or longer. Mail questionnaires also do not suffer from the disadvantage of respondent fatigue, as the questionnaire can be completed at the respondent's leisure over several sittings if necessary. Similarly, complicated questions, especially those that require the respondent to see or read something, are extremely difficult via the telephone, whereas such items may work quite well in both personal interviews and in mail questionnaires.

In sum, I am not suggesting that a telephone survey is always the method of choice, but these are the major considerations that lead me to conclude that telephone surveying is a very attractive approach to gathering precise estimates on many topics of interest.

THE TELEPHONE SURVEY PHENOMENON IN THE UNITED STATES

There are two sets of factors concerning the phenomenon of the telephone that directly affect the successful (i.e., valid) conduct of telephone surveys. First there are "hardware" factors that physically determine the ability to reach respondents via telephone. Second there are social factors related to the verbal and nonverbal behavior of persons contacted via telephone. This section will address only some of these physical and social factors. Readers interested in more information should turn to de Sola Pool's (1977) volume, *The Social Impact of the Telephone,* and Brooks's (1976) book, *Telephone: The First Hundred Years,* along with Frey's (1983) more detailed coverage of the telephone phenomenon as it specifically relates to telephone surveying.

Physical Factors

Interconnection of telephone lines. By the mid-1940s virtually every residential and business telephone in the United States was interconnected, at least indirectly, through the Bell network (Pierce, 1977). Before then it would have been impossible for telephone interviewers at some central location to reach all households in the United States that had a telephone because independent telephone companies did not fully connect. Thus pockets of the nation would have remained unsampled. With the removal of this barrier it finally became theoretically possible for a telephone survey of the United States to reach any household with a telephone, regardless of where interviewers were calling *from* or where they were calling *to.*

The saturation of telephone lines in households. Yet even with the removal of this barrier, the prevalence of households with telephones in the United States in the 1940s was too sparse to justify fully the use of the telephone for drawing a valid (representative) sample of the population. Within the last 20 years this has changed.

By 1960 approximately 80% of all households had a telephone. By 1965 telephone saturation had increased to 85%, and by 1970 it was over 90% (U.S. Bureau of the Census, 1984).

As of the early 1980s there were approximately 182 million telephones in the United States. Only Sweden has a greater person-to-telephone ratio among the developed countries of the world (AT&T, 1982). Of all these American telephones, nearly 75%, or 134 million, were residential units. This 3:1 ratio of residential-to-nonresidential telephones is very similar to what was found by Groves and Kahn (1979) in their 1976 telephone samplings of the United States.

The most recent estimates of the proportion of U.S. households with at least one telephone access line suggest that the figure is above 95%. (A telephone access line refers to each unique telephone number.) AT&T puts that figure at 97% as of 1982; the U.S. Federal Communications Commission listed it at 96% in 1981; and Frey (1983) estimates it at 98%. Given the variations of different estimates, a conservative figure would put the percentage at *at least* 95% as of 1986.

This estimate of "at least 95%" is also consistent with the findings of Groves and Kahn in their 1976 comparison of personal interview surveying and telephone surveying. In that study they found that only 7% of their personal interview national probability sample of households had no telephone service. As would be expected, those households without telephones were not a mirror image of the entire sample—at least not from a demographic standpoint.

Compared to the general population sampled by Groves and Kahn, those without telephones were more likely to be in single adult households, considerably less educated, poorer, minorities, and employed as nonprofessional and nonmanagerial workers. It is worth noting, however, that on many attitudinal questions those in housholds without telephones as a group did not differ to any great extent from the rest of the population as a whole.

For those conducting telephone surveys in local areas, it is important to recognize that the proportion of households with at least one telephone access line within a given area is not entirely uniform throughout the United States. As shown in Table 1, according to the most recently available statistics, in 13 states at least 99% of all households are estimated to have telephone service. In contrast, in 12 states fewer

TABLE 1
Telephone Saturation of Households by State, 1981

State	Percentage Households with Service	State	Percentage Households with Service
Entire U. S.	96	Missouri	94
Alabama	87	Montana	95
Alaska	90	Nebraska	100
Arizona	95	Nevada	84
Arkansas	85	New Hampshire	99
California	100	New Jersey	100
Colorado	97	New Mexico	86
Connecticut	100	New York	97
Delaware	100	North Carolina	91
District of Columbia	100	North Dakota	98
Florida	98	Ohio	94
Georgia	88	Oklahoma	96
Hawaii	98	Oregon	86
Idaho	92	Pennsylvania	99
Illinois	99	Rhode Island	98
Indiana	92	South Carolina	86
Iowa	95	South Dakota	92
Kansas	96	Tennessee	88
Kentucky	86	Texas	95
Louisiana	93	Utah	93
Maine	98	Vermont	100
Maryland	99	Virginia	91
Massachusetts	100	Washington	90
Michigan	98	West Virginia	85
Minnesota	99	Wisconsin	98
Mississippi	82	Wyoming	89

than 90% of the households have telephones. Someone planning a local or regional telephone survey of the general population must know in advance the prevalence of telephones within the sampling boundaries. Then, with paramount consideration given to the nature of the survey topic, an informed a priori decision can be made regarding the validity of choosing a telephone survey over personal interviewing.

The future saturation of U.S. households with telephone access lines is somewhat uncertain. Prior to the 1984 AT&T divestiture there were worries that the cost of local telephone service (i.e., the monthly charge to have equipment and an access line) would skyrocket. Had this happened, it is very likely that the proportion of households in the

United States with telephone access lines would have decreased. To be safe telephone surveyors will need to watch future developments in the residential telephone market.

Multiple-line households. A final issue regarding the physical factors that affect surveying via telephone is that of *multiple-line* households. This has an effect on telephone sampling opposite to that created by households without service. Whenever a random number dialing scheme is used for sampling, households with more than one telephone number will have a greater probability of being sampled than the more typical household with only one access line. (Note that this issue is not one of having multiple extension telephones on the same number. The problem involves households that have two or more different telephone numbers.)

Groves and Kahn (1979) found that approximately 5% of their national samples of households with telephone service reported having more than one number (the vast majority of these multiple-line households reported having two different numbers). These figures also vary on a regional basis. For example, surveys conducted by the Northwestern University Survey Laboratory in the Chicago metropolitan area consistently find 12%-15% of households reporting more than one telephone number, which corresponds closely with Illinois Bell estimates.

Other physical factors. There remain other types of variations in telephone companies' services and policies throughout the nation that can affect the planning and conduct of telephone surveys. This is not surprising with the more than 60 telephone companies currently offering local service (U.S. Bureau of the Census, 1984). For example, telephone companies have different procedures for opening up working banks of suffixes (i.e., the last four digits of the telephone number). Local companies also vary greatly in the cooperation they give to telephone survey researchers. Another problem is the manner in which different telephone companies handle nonworking numbers, which is a special problem for telephone surveys that employ random-digit dialing. What all this means is that experience with a telephone survey in one geographic region may not necessarily generalize when sampling in another region.

Social Factors

With the theoretical possibility of being able to reach nearly all U.S. households via the telephone, it is worth considering the social environment in which telephone surveys operate. As Frey (1983) points out, there are several "behavioral norms" regarding the telephone that generally work to the advantage of telephone interviewers. Regardless of whether all persons living in the United States grew up in households with telephones, exposure to the telephone in the home has been so high since World War II that nearly all members of American society share these norms.

A ringing telephone will be answered. Though often taken for granted, the most important of these norms is that a ringing telephone will almost always be answered, provided someone is there. Granted, there is considerable variation from household to household and from person to person in how quickly a telephone is answered. Experience shows that if a telephone is answered, the median number of rings it takes is about three or four, and more than 90% of the time it will be answered within seven to eight rings. Thus there is no problem of persons allowing ringing telephones to go unanswered, which would lessen the validity of telephone surveying if people did behave in this manner.

Protocol for terminating a telephone conversation. A second, less obvious norm also works to the advantage of telephone surveying. As Frey (1983) observes, it is implicit in a telephone conversation that it is the caller who determines the duration of the verbal interaction. That is, the caller had some purpose in placing the call, and courtesy dictates that that purpose should be fulfilled before the call is terminated. Obviously, not all persons practice this courtesy when they answer their telephone; otherwise telephone interviewers would not be refused, especially with those occasional "hang-ups without comment." Nevertheless, this latter problem is not a typical occurrence and may be one disproportionately associated with non-English-speaking households.

Judging veracity. Another assumption about the interviewer-respondent interaction that underlies the validity of telephone surveying is that of *veracity.* A naive criticism of telephone interviewing argues that respondents often lie when they are interviewed via telephone, thereby invalidating the data. My own research (Lavrakas & Maier, 1979; Maier & Lavrakas, 1976), and that of others (e.g., Ekman & Friesen, 1974, 1976; Maier, 1966; Maier & Thurber, 1968) suggests the existence of a general ability of listeners (e.g., interviewers) to "sense" accurately the veracity of another person when listening to his or her voice. In fact, this research also suggests that in-person interviewing may be more susceptible to deception, as visual cues are more likely to confuse an untrained judge of another's veracity.

Furthermore, logic dictates that few respondents would waste their own time in order purposely to trick a telephone interviewer; people so disposed are more likely simply to refuse the interview. All things considered, it is a safe assumption that in most instances most respondents provide reasonably accurate information when queried in telephone surveys.

Summary

There currently are no insurmountable barriers in the United States of either a physical or social nature that automatically invalidate the use of telephone surveys for the purpose of gathering representative data from the general population. On the physical side, however, not until the 1970s could telephone survey research be defended as being capable of gathering data with high external validity (i.e., generalizability). This is not to say that telephone surveys are always justified, but telephone surveying no longer deserves a reputation as being inferior to in-person interviewing from the standpoint of either sampling or asking questions.

BASIC STEPS IN THE
TELEPHONE SURVEY PROCESS

The following are the steps that are typically performed when conducting a *quality* telephone survey that is not done via computer-assisted telephone interviewing (CATI):

(1) deciding upon a sampling design, including the method of respondent selection within a sampling unit;

    (2) developing and formatting a draft questionnaire;

    (3) choosing a method to generate the pool of telephone numbers that will be used in sampling;

    (4) producing a call-sheet for each number that will be used in sampling;

    (5) developing a draft introduction/selection sheet and fallback statements for use by interviewers;

    (6) hiring interviewers and supervisors, and scheduling interviewing sessions;

    (7) pilot-testing and revising survey instruments;

    (8) printing final questionnaires and other forms;

    (9) training interviewers and supervisors; and

  (10) conducting fully supervised interviews.

The first step in the telephone survey process is to choose a sampling design. This choice requires determining who will be sampled and *how* the sampling design will be implemented. This includes decisions about the area in which sampling will occur and the method that will be used to produce a sampling pool (i.e., those numbers that will be used to reach respondents). Each of these telephone numbers eventually must be printed on a separate call-sheet that will allow supervisory personnel to control the sampling process.

A draft questionnaire must be written and then formatted in as convenient to use manner as possible so that interviewers' work will be facilitated. The sampling design will partly determine the nature and wording of questionnaire items. Along with a draft introductory "spiel" and any respondent selection sequence that must be used to sample respondents from within sampling units, the draft questionnaire should be pilot-tested to identify potential problems and to estimate the average time it takes to complete. This can usually be accomplished with 25-50 "practice" interviews.

After the pilot test, a debriefing session can be held to identify any changes that need to be made before printing final copies of the questionnaire and other survey forms. Supervisory personnel and interviewers must be hired and decisions must be made about the scheduling of interviewing sessions. Training sessions should be held for supervisors and interviewers.

Interviewing then begins under highly controlled conditions. Supervisors immediately validate completed interviews and listen in on ongoing interviewing, providing feedback to interviewers as necessary.

CONTENTS AND ORGANIZATION
OF THIS TEXT

The purpose of this text is to assist persons who do not consider themselves expert in planning and executing telephone surveys. Specifically, this book addresses the following aspects of telephone surveys in detail:

(1) generating and processing telephone survey sampling pools;
(2) selecting a respondent and securing cooperation; and
(3) structuring the work of interviewers and supervisors.

This text is intended to fit into the series of Sage books on research methods that already includes Floyd J. Fowler's book on general survey research, *Survey Research Methods* (1984). It takes a "how-to" approach to sampling, respondent selection, and supervision.

Issues Not Addressed

The text will not address in any detail

(1) how a survey fits into a larger research project;
(2) the wording of questionnaire items;
(3) a discussion of sources of "error" and their estimation;
(4) a review of the ethics of survey research;
(5) the analysis of survey data; and
(6) computer-assisted telephone interviewing (CATI).

The larger research project. A person should be exposed to a general social science methods course or textbook (e.g., Babbie, 1983; Crano & Brewer, 1973) before undertaking a survey, be it with face-to-face interviews, mail questionnaires, or via telephone. Only with an adequate appreciation for social science can the strengths and limits of surveys be understood. This text assumes that one has done this preliminary homework, has decided that a telephone survey is the preferred mode of data collection (or is trying to make this decision), and wants to learn more about conducting one.

Developing questionnaire items. The limited scope of this text makes it impossible to give any attention to the generation and refinement of questionnaire items. Comprehensive treatment of these issues is presented elsewhere (e.g., Belson, 1981; Robinson & Shaver, 1973; Schuman & Presser, 1981; Sudman & Bradburn, 1982). When using other textbooks for assistance in item construction, it is also recommended that consideration be given to developing multi-item scales and indices through the use of factor analysis and reliability checks on internal consistency (e.g., see Dawes, 1972).

Estimating survey error. The calculation of estimates of precision (i.e., a survey's "margin of error") is not addressed in this book. These estimates focus mostly on the magnitude of the imprecision that results when estimates are based on a sample or subset of an entire population, even when sampling is truly random. As discussed by Fowler (1984), however, sampling error is *only one source* of Total Survey Error, and the reader is encouraged to review that book in this context.

Survey ethics. Both Fowler (1984) and Frey (1983) cover a variety of ethical issues in survey research; for example, standards on disclosure of results and informed consent. In this text discussion will be limited to ethical guidelines for interviewing, though in most instances such guidelines are based on a surveyor's own professional judgment. That is, what one person may view as "persistent persuasion" on the part of an interviewer may be judged as somewhat rude or overly aggressive interviewing by another.

Data analysis. Covering the analysis of survey data requires a textbook in itself. Survey data lend themselves to all types of statistical analyses. Contrary to what some persons believe, surveys do not gather a "special kind" of data that require special statistical procedures. Surveys are *methodological* techniques, not statistical ones.

A special statistical procedure that is sometimes used to analyze survey data is "weighting"—that is, a post hoc adjustment of data to estimate more precisely the population from which the sample was drawn. The present text does not address this issue.

Computer-assisted telephone interviewing (CATI). With the ready availability of microcomputers, more and more telephone surveys will be conducted by interviewers sitting at a computer terminal. The computer has the potential to generate and control the sample, to dial the telephone number, to lead the interviewer through the respondent selection process and through the entire questionnaire, and to compile the data as they are gathered.

For many reasons CATI systems are extremely attractive and are the future of telephone interviewing. As stated in the preface, this text is meant for those persons who do not have access to CATI systems and thus must employ primarily a paper-and-pencil approach to telephone surveying.

Using This Text to Help
Plan a Telephone Survey

Of the various steps that make up the telephone survey process, this text provides detailed assistance in deciding upon the following:

(1) What telephone numbers will form the sampling pool?
(2) How will these numbers be processed and controlled?
(3) How will an eligible respondent be chosen?
(4) How to choose and train interviewers?
(5) What quality control methods will be employed to structure and monitor interviewing?

Generating telephone survey sampling pools. Chapter 2 explains how to produce a set of telephone numbers for use in sampling. The first decision one is faced with is whether to draw telephone numbers from a list (e.g., a telephone directory) or to use some technique for randomly generating telephone numbers. This decision should never be made for the mere sake of convenience.

There are instances in which list sampling is quite appropriate—for example, whenever some "special" group of persons, such as pediatricians or clients of a public service agency, make up the population of interest. It is unnecessary, foolish, and typically inappropriate to employ randomly generated telephone numbers in such instances, unless the "density" of the group in the general population is high enough to maintain an acceptable level of interviewer productivity. These considerations are discussed in Chapter 2.

There are many instances in which list sampling of the general population would be acceptable for a researcher who has no interest in generalizing to the population at large but, rather, is looking for "within-person" interrelationships. For example, if a researcher wanted to determine the intercorrelation of foot size with a predisposition toward aggression, sampling from a telephone directory is unlikely to bias the results.

Conversely, list sampling for general population surveys is rarely appropriate if one plans to generalize sample results to the total population. The only exception to this may be in certain rural areas, where nearly all residents list their telephone numbers in the local directory and population ingress is so low as to alleviate worry about new listings that are missing from the most recent telephone book. In most general population surveys, however, some form of random-digit dialing (hereafter referred to as RDD) should be employed. There are a number of different RDD choices, as described in Chapter 2.

Controlling sampling pools. Once a researcher has determined the method by which the sampling pool of telephone numbers will be generated, attention next focuses on the process by which the dialing of these numbers will be organized and controlled. Persons naive to this aspect of telephone surveying may assume that interviewers simply dial one number after another until the desired sample size is attained. As discussed in Chapter 3, tight control over the "processing" of the sampling pool is a necessary condition for quality (i.e., representative) results. Chapter 3 presents a highly structured, paper-and-pencil, hand-sorted approach to controlling a telephone survey sampling pool.

Choosing an eligible respondent. Chapter 4 addresses the second stage of the interviewing process, gaining the compliance of the properly selected respondent. Here again, persons naive to quality telephone survey methods seem to assume that interviewers simply administer the questionnaire to the first person who answers the telephone, not recognizing that gender and age biases can often result when such a procedure is followed.

In some instances, respondent selection is a *fait accompli*, as when one is directly sampling respondents *by name* from a list. But in other instances telephone numbers provide the entré, and names of preselected respondents are not known. When this happens it is most likely that a surveyor will want to employ a systematic selection procedure in order to avoid the bias that could occur from respondent selection solely at the discretion of interviewers. Systematic respondent selection procedures increase the representativeness (external validity) of the final sample.

Interviewers and supervision. Chapters 5 and 6 discuss the training and supervision of interviewers. Good telephone interviewers appear to have a natural aptitude for the work. Thus the recruitment, training, and supervisory procedures that one utilizes should ideally screen for and certainly reinforce this aptitude. While training prior to the start of actual surveying is desirable, necessary, and important, routine *on-the-job* training is even more critical, as explained in Chapter 5.

There should be no doubt that the control afforded by centralized telephone interviewing over the interviewing process is one of the most compelling reasons for choosing telephone surveying whenever it is appropriate for one's sampling design. The supervisory routine that is instituted over the interviewing process may be the most critical aspect for producing quality telephone surveys. Chapter 6 discusses the supervisory duties that occur throughout the steps in the survey process.

Appendices. Appendix A presents an SPSS computer program for generating random-digit dialing sampling pools as discussed in Chapter 2. Appendix B provides advice on the formatting of telephone survey questionnaires so as to help make the questionnaire as easy for interviewers to use as possible. Appendix C lists companies that market *reverse telephone directories*, directories that list telephone numbers by addresses and by numerical order rather than by alphabetized last names. These directories are especially helpful to anyone planning a telephone survey of the general population in a relatively confined geographical area (e.g., a city, county, or metropolitan area).

Summary

Although market researchers, academics, the media, and federal government agencies traditionally have been associated with the conduct of surveys, I believe we are entering an era in which survey data will be collected to aid all sorts of decisions made by less technical decision makers in both the public and private sectors. This text is explicitly written with such an "applied" audience in mind. It is meant to help nonexperts conduct good (reliable) telephone surveys. It assumes that the vast majority of those doing telephone surveys in the 1980s will *not* have access to a computer-assisted telephone interviewing system.

ADDITIONAL SOURCES OF INSTRUCTION
ON SURVEY METHODOLOGIES

Other textbooks cover the topics of sampling, selection, and supervision in telephone surveys, but none covers them with as detailed a "how-to" perspective as the present text. For the most part my approach to telephone surveying is similar to that of others (e.g., Frey, 1983; Dillman, 1978). But in my judgment no other author places as much explicit emphasis on the importance of *constant and intense supervision* of the entire telephone surveying process.

Furthermore, most other authors of survey methods textbooks developed their own expertise from experience with household probability sampling for use with face-to-face interviewing. I believe that this legacy of experience with personal interviewing occasionally yields a somewhat negative disposition toward telephone surveying, which is carried forward in the tone of some other textbooks.

Due to its length, this text cannot cover all aspects of the telephone survey process. This is especially true for questionnaire development. Thus this chapter finishes with a brief review of additional sources I recommend to those interested in expanding their knowledge base.

General Survey Methods

Ideally one should have a broad understanding of survey methods, not merely those related to a specific mode of data collection (e.g., via telephone). Babbie's (1983) text, *The Practice of Social Research*, does a very good job of putting traditional survey methodology in perspective with other methodological approaches. *Survey Research Methods* by Fowler (1984) provides a comprehensive overview of almost all issues that confront survey researchers, as well as dealing with important topics that have received relatively little coverage elsewhere. Dillman's (1978) book, *Mail and Telephone Surveys: The Total Design Method*, is a very detailed presentation of the author's own tailored approach to survey research. Finally, Frey's (1983) text, *Survey Research by Telephone*, is strongly recommended because of the broadly focused perspective on telephone surveying it offers.

Sampling

From a statistical standpoint, Cochran's (1977) *Sampling Techniques* presents an exhaustive treatment of sampling theory for survey research. From a more applied but nevertheless comprehensive perspective, Sudman's (1976) text, *Applied Sampling*, should be consulted. A more dated but extremely comprehensive and still useful text is *Survey Sampling* by Kish (1965). This book is "dated" in the sense that it was written before random-digit dialing was an accepted sampling technique). Finally, Henry's forthcoming text, *Practical Sampling,* presents an applied guide for the novice surveyor.

Question Formulation

Although the construction of valid questionnaire items includes the use of scientific methods, the process is still very much a craft and also somewhat of an art. Texts exist that teach the systematic steps that should be followed in developing new items for surveys. Yet the exact wording that is decided upon will often rest on the professional judgment of the individual surveyor. Of course, over the years many standardized questions and scales have been devised by others and should be consulted and used whenever possible (i.e., there's no reason to reinvent the wheel). On the other hand, I am not suggesting that there is no room for improving on traditional items.

Sudman and Bradburn have collaborated on three books that focus on various aspects of questionnaire design: *Response Effects in Surveys* (1974), *Improving Interview Method and Questionnaire Design* (1979), and *Asking Questions* (1982). Schuman and Presser's (1981) text, *Questions and Answers in Attitude Surveys*, can also be recommended for its very thorough treatment of survey item formulation. When searching for a collection of items that have been at least partially validated, books from the Institute for Social Research at the University of Michigan, such as Robinson and Shaver's (1973) *Measures of Social Psychological Attitudes,* can be consulted. Finally, Edwards's forthcoming text, *Self-Report Measures of Knowledge, Attitudes and Behavior,* will be valuable for its applied focus.

Methodological Periodicals

A final source that should be regularly checked by those interested in telephone survey methods is the literature that is published in scholarly journals. *Public Opinion Quarterly* and the *Journal of Marketing Research* are two sources that often contain the better methodological articles on telephone surveying and survey methods in general. Each is likely to be available at any university library.

EXERCISES

1. Review at least one other textbook that discusses the advantages and disadvantages of telephone surveys compared to other forms of surveying. Write a two-page paper comparing the position taken in the present text with that of the other author(s).

2. Call your local telephone company and try to get information about the number of residential access lines in some local municipality and the proportion of unlisted telephone numbers in that municipality. In dealing with the company representatives be polite yet persistent (if necessary). Regardless of whether you get the information, write a short paper describing the nature of the assistance (or lack of it) you received from the telephone company representatives. (If you are given the information you request please send a thank-you letter to the person who helped you.)

3. Develop a comprehensive time line for conducting a telephone survey, starting with the choice of a sampling design. Assume interviewing will last three weeks.

4. Find and review a recent article on telephone survey methods (i.e., not merely an article about a survey that was conducted via telephone) from either *Public Opinion Quarterly* or the *Journal of Marketing Research*. Write a two-page summary of the article.

2

GENERATING SAMPLING POOLS

A sampling pool for a telephone survey is the set of telephone numbers that will be used by interviewers in the course of trying to complete a predetermined number of interviews (the survey's sample size). There are many techniques for generating sampling pools, as reviewed in this chapter. All techniques can be generated by computer or manually. Depending on the particulars of a survey, either approach may prove preferable. It remains up to the individual surveyor to make an informed decision regarding the way in which the sampling pool will be generated and how large a sampling pool is likely to be required.

The purpose of this chapter is to familiarize the reader with various techniques for generating a telephone survey sampling pool. A sampling pool is the entire set of telephone numbers that will be used by interviewers to attain the desired number of completions. When a surveyor does not have a CATI system to generate and control the telephone numbers used in the survey, he or she should generate the entire sampling pool before interviewing begins.

The chapter begins with a discussion of the considerations that go into choosing a valid sampling design in telephone surveys. This decision must be made before deciding how to generate the sampling pool, because the sampling design guides the surveyor in generating the sampling pool. Once a sampling design is chosen the decision is made whether to generate the sampling pool via list sampling or through random-digit dialing and whether to do this manually or to use a computer. Several approaches to these various techniques are discussed. The chapter concludes by answering the question of *how large* a sampling pool to generate. (Chapter 2 focuses only on the generation of sampling pools; Chapter 3 deals with the processing of the telephone numbers that have been generated.)

CHOOSING A VALID SAMPLING DESIGN

In deciding upon a valid sampling design and the method one will employ to operationalize that design for telephone surveys, a surveyor must simultaneously consider the following:

(1) What is the purpose of the survey?
(2) Who, demographically speaking, will be sampled?
(3) How prevalent are "missing" telephone numbers?
(4) What resources are available to support the survey?

Purpose of the Survey

The purpose of a survey is the paramount factor in determining the adequacy of a sampling design. Most persons considering the use of a telephone survey (or any survey) will have one of three purposes in mind.

Measuring population parameters. A surveyor may want to determine the level to which some variable exists within a population. For example, what proportion of residents in a city are afraid to leave their homes at night? Or, what is the percentage of households with smoke detectors? In these cases it is of utmost importance that a sampling design be chosen that comes as close as possible to pure random selection from the larger population so as to ensure the representativeness, and thus validity, of the gathered data.

When this is the purpose of a survey, the primary consideration is the *generalizability* of the sample, or what social science methodologists call the survey's "external validity" (see Campbell & Stanley, 1963; Cook & Campbell, 1979) In most instances if a sample is meant to estimate the level at which some variable exists within a population and the sampling design does not have high external validity, there can be little justification for its use. When respondents are sampled in an uncontrolled, unsystematic manner there is no way to estimate the survey's degree of precision (i.e., margin of error). Without an estimate of statistical precision, a survey cannot be considered scientific, at least not for the purposes of making estimates on the prevalence of some variable of interest.

A lack of external validity typically results when mail surveys and call-in telephone polling are used, for example, to measure voting intentions or attitudes toward social issues. An example of this occurred while this book was being written. A radio station in Chicago sponsored a call-in telephone poll to determine whether more persons backed Chicago's mayor or his city council opponents. Nearly 30,000 calls were made to one of two "900" telephone numbers to register preference. Of these calls 75% supported the mayor's opponents. A few weeks later the Northwestern University Survey Laboratory conducted a telephone survey of the metropolitan Chicago area using RDD (n = 450) and *scientifically* determined that about four out of ten area residents supported the mayor, only two of ten backed his opponents, and the remainder sided with neither faction. These results were very different from the uncontrolled and thus unreliable (i.e., inaccurate) sampling method used by the radio station.

Estimating multivariate relationships. If a survey is not meant to estimate the level to which a variable exists in the population but rather to study interrelationships *among* variables, pure random sampling may be less important. In the case of someone interested in measuring the correlation between fear of crime, age, race, and gender, a sampling design that ensures a heterogeneous sample but not necessarily a random one may well suffice. Here the purpose of the survey would not be to estimate the proportion of the population that was fearful, but rather what types of persons were most or least fearful.

Evaluation research. A third purpose for which a survey may be needed is that of evaluation research (see Weiss, 1972). For example, if an evaluator conducted a panel study (a survey in which the same respondents were interviewed at two or more points in time) to determine the effect of a community crime prevention program on residents' fear of crime, it may not be necessary to draw a truly random sample of the population of interest at Wave 1, as it is *change* in fear of crime that is being investigated (Lavrakas & Tyler, 1983). This reasoning assumes that the variable of interest is not confounded with the types of persons who were sampled. If it were confounded, as in the case in which a new recreation program was being evaluated but the sampling design undersampled those persons most likely to be affected by the program (e.g., persons under 30 years of age), the evaluator would need to choose a sampling design that yielded a more representative sample.

Summary. The purpose of the telephone survey, then, will often determine whether some form of RDD is called for or whether an existing list can be used from which to sample. If the purpose is to estimate some univariate "population parameter" in the general population, then RDD will almost always be the sampling design of choice. On the other hand, if a telephone survey is meant to estimate a "population parameter" of some small subset of the general population (e.g., all members of the American Medical Association), then random list sampling would certainly be preferable.

Who Will Be Sampled?

The practical matter of *who* will be interviewed may also influence the choice of sampling design, especially from a cost standpoint. If a survey needs to sample some small subset of the general population, then often a list will exist that will provide at least a marginally representative sampling. For example, if female nurses are the desired respondents, then representative lists of nurses need to be gathered from which to draw a preliminary sample, with gender being screened in the survey's introduction. In contrast, if working women in the general population define the set of eligible respondents, then an RDD survey that subsequently screens for employed females would be the method of choice, given that as many as one-half of all households may contain an eligible respondent.

Problems arise when sampling must be restricted to relatively small geographic boundaries, such as when sampling only in certain neighborhoods. In this instance RDD sampling will rarely be cost-acceptable; in other words, interviewers would reach a very large proportion of ineligible households because telephone prefixes rarely conform to neighborhood boundaries. In this case if the survey's purpose is to estimate neighborhood-level parameters, then telephone sampling may prove unacceptable. In contrast, if it can be reasoned that one need not be concerned about missing residents who live in households with unlisted telephone numbers, then the use of a reverse directory should solve the problem. Unfortunately, this will never be the preferred approach if one wants a sampling of opinion with high external validity.

Prevalence of Missing Numbers

Assuming that sampling will be done of the public at large and that the purpose of the survey is to estimate univariate population parameters, then the proportion of households with unlisted telephone numbers and the residential mobility within the sampling area can influence the decision of whether to use some form of RDD or to sample randomly from a directory or other listing. Experience shows that surveys designed to gather valid estimates of univariate population parameters in large cities will almost always require RDD, given that as many as half of all residential telephone numbers will not be published in the current directory. In smaller cities and suburbs the proportion of telephone numbers that are missing from the local directory decreases, whereas in many rural areas it may be so low as to eliminate the need to consider RDD seriously.

To make an informed decision about directory sampling versus RDD, one needs a good estimate of the proportion of households whose numbers are not published. Sometimes local telephone companies will provide this information, but often they will not. In the latter instance a surveyor must estimate this proportion. One approach to estimation is to determine the approximate number of telephone numbers in the local directory and compare it to census statistics on the number of households in the sampling area. Although there are no accepted standards here, I would recommend against directory sampling if the proportion of missing numbers is estimated to be greater than 10%-15%. Again, the reader is reminded that this problem is usually not an issue unless the survey's purpose is to estimate the level to which a variable exists in the general population.

Availability of Resources

A final consideration, but not necessarily the least important, is the amount of resources (including person time and computer time) available for generating sampling pools and for interviewing. Both list sampling and RDD sampling can be done by hand or by computer. The size of the sampling pool that needs to be generated and the size of the final sample that will be interviewed must be considered here. For example, if a sample size of 2,000 respondents will be interviewed, and the purpose of the survey is to study the interrelationships of variables and not to estimate population parameters for single variables, then a computer-generated RDD sample may still be preferred over a hand-drawn directory sample, from the standpoint of the reduced person time it would take to generate the sampling pool via computer versus manually. On the other hand, if approximately 15% of the population is missing from a recent directory and rough estimates of population values are acceptable, then directory sampling may be the preferred choice for someone who cannot afford the additional interviewing time that would be likely to be needed using RDD.

For the most part, then, each decision on what type of sampling should be done for a survey is a unique one. It is definitely not an arbitrary one and often requires compromises. These trade-offs have to do with sacrificing some degree of precision for the purposes of feasibility. The extent to which one can sacrifice precision and still gather useful (i.e., essentially valid) data is certainly debatable. Whatever is decided, the surveyor must be able to defend the sampling decision.

RANDOM-DIGIT DIALING (RDD)

Random-digit dialing is a group of techniques that theoretically provide an equal probability of reaching a household with a telephone access line (i.e., a unique telephone number that rings in that household only) regardless of whether its telephone number is published or listed. In practice the notion of equal probability applies only to those households with one telephone access line. For those households with two or more telephone lines, adjustments must sometimes be made in weighting one's final data to correct for the greater probability of sampling such households. Once again, the need for such adjustments will depend on the survey's purpose.

A fairly sizable proportion of the American public, though not yet a majority, has unpublished (not printed in a local telephone directory but accessible through Directory Information) or unlisted (not accessible at all) telephone numbers. This proportion appears to be growing, and for psychological reasons it can be expected to continue to increase, especially in urban areas where those most likely to have unlisted telephone numbers typically live. Despite the often held assumption that those who do not list their telephone numbers live in upper-income white households, it is lower-income minority Americans who, as a group, are most likely to have unlisted telephone numbers.

A general rule is that the farther one samples from central cities, the lower the proportion of households with unlisted telephone numbers. Thus inner-ring suburbs typically will have a lower proportion of unlisted telephone numbers than in a central city itself. Outer-ring suburbs will have even lower levels, and as one moves into rural areas the "unlisted phenomenon" dwindles. For example, about 50% of all City of Chicago households have unlisted numbers; in inner-ring suburbs of Chicago such as Evanston, this drops to 20%-30%. As one moves further away from Chicago city limits, outer-ring suburbs show a 10%-20% unlisted rate. In essentially rural areas it often drops below 5%.

Unlisted telephone numbers are a barrier to valid sampling when a survey's purpose is to estimate the level that certain variables exist in the general population. This results because it is not a random subset of the general population that chooses not to list telephone numbers. As mentioned above, income is generally inversely related to nonlisting. We have also found that women, single adults, and those with relatively less education are more likely not to list their telephone numbers. Not surprisingly, greater fear of crime is directly related to having an unlisted telephone number (Lavrakas et al., 1980).

RDD breaks through the barrier to high external validity caused by unlisted telephone numbers. Once a surveyor knows the prefixes (i.e., the first three digits in a local telephone number) that ring within the sampling boundaries, various techniques can be used to add random four-digit suffixes to produce seven-digit telephone numbers that may or may not be working and, if working, may or may not ring in households *regardless of whether the number is listed.* (For telephone surveys that cross area codes, ten-digit numbers must be used.)

When it has been decided that some form of RDD sampling will take place, the pool of numbers that will be processed by interviewers can be generated by hand or by computer. It is almost always preferable to do this by computer, but it is not necessary to do so. Theoretically, any approach to generating RDD sampling pools by computer can be used by hand. In practice, however, it is often much too time consuming to justify the manual approach. Appendix A contains a listing of an SPSS program that generates RDD sampling pools (LeBailly & Lavrakas, 1981). With the growing prevalence of microcomputers, a surveyor could easily adapt the structure that underlies this SPSS routine for use in BASIC or with other computer languages.

Getting Ready for Generating
Most RDD Sampling Pools

Gathering telephone prefixes. The first step in generating a sampling pool for most RDD techniques is to assemble an exhaustive list of prefixes that ring within the geographic boundaries of the sampling area. Unfortunately, this is often not a straightforward or easy task. Sometimes the boundaries of the sampling area and the boundaries of the prefixes that ring in the sampling area coincide exactly. Sometimes boundaries of telephone prefixes coincide somewhat closely with the geographic perimeter of the desired sampling area. In other cases the prefix boundaries do not at all approximate the sampling area's boundaries. In this latter instance RDD sampling may have to be ruled out as too costly, which in turn may negate the value of the survey. In the former instance, if the prefix boundaries are fairly close to the boundaries of the preferred sampling area, it is possible to use screening questions to exclude those who live outside the sampling area, or, instead, one may choose to shrink or expand the sampling area to conform to the perimeter defined by the prefixes. As always, these are not arbitrary decisions, and it remains the responsibility of the surveyor to determine the extent to which the survey's purpose might be compromised.

The help that one can expect from local telephone companies in providing information about telephone prefixes will vary. The easiest approach is knowing someone who works for the telephone company who will provide the prefix information being sought. Apart from this, an individual's own creative perseverance will often yield prefix information from the telephone company that a less persistent surveyor cannot obtain.

If the telephone company chooses not to help, all is not lost. By using a reverse directory or even a regular telephone directory one can gather fairly precise estimates of the information originally sought from the telephone company. Using a reverse directory is easier, because the expressed purpose of such volumes is to present telephone numbers by geographical order. Furthermore, some publishers of reverse directories also provide aggregate statistics, such as the number of listed residential accounts on each prefix. Appendix D contains a listing of reverse directory publishers for many large population centers in the United States and Canada.

When a reverse directory is not available the task is more time consuming and sometimes simply not feasible. By assembling all the local telephone directories that serve the sampling area, a surveyor can methodically determine the match between prefixes and the perimeter of the sampling area. This is done using a map to plot systematically the location of prefixes based on the addresses found in the telephone directories. Depending upon the size of one's sampling area, this can be an extremely time-consuming process. In fact, for anything but a relatively small local area, this approach is quite impractical.

Determining the number of lines per prefix. As will be discussed later in more detail, it is also useful to know something about the number of residential telephone access lines in operation for each prefix in the sampling area. This information can be used to generate random telephone numbers in the proportion that each prefix exists within the sampling area; in this way the final sample will be *stratified* by prefix. Ideally this information can be retrieved from the telephone companies servicing the sampling area. But if one has to rely on regular telephone directories for these data, it is possible to sample prefixes systematically from a representative sample of pages within directories to estimate the relative proportion of residential telephones associated with the various prefixes that will be used.

For example, in the city of Evanston, Illinois there are seven residential prefixes. By sampling telephone numbers from pages in the Evanston directory one would learn that three of these prefixes are used for two-thirds of all residential access lines. When generating an RDD sampling pool for Evanston, it is most efficient (from the standpoint of interviewer processing time) to use a sampling pool that reflects this distribution of prefixes. This approach is quite feasible when sampling is confined to relatively small geographical areas.

Identifying nonworking banks of suffixes. Information about vacuous banks of suffixes (numerical ranges of telephone numbers that do not operate or contain no residential access lines) can also be used to improve the efficiency of an RDD sampling pool. If this type of information is not readily forthcoming from the telephone company, a reverse directory can be used. By closely scanning the numerically ordered listing of each prefix one can find ranges of vacuous suffixes. The validity of this method hinges on the fact that telephone companies generally do not assign unlisted telephone numbers from special banks of suffixes. Instead, an available telephone number is first assigned to a new customer, *then* the company determines whether the customer wants the number published or listed. Thus by "eyeballing" the numerically ordered listing of telephone numbers in a reverse directory, one can methodically determine which banks of suffixes are operational. I recommend that the metric used in this search be in ranges of 100—that is, the surveyor should try to determine whether numbers exist in the 0000-0099 bank, the 0100-0199 bank, the 0200-0299 bank, and so on for each prefix.

This can be an onerous task when the sampling area contains hundreds of prefixes, but using such information will significantly reduce the proportion of nonworking numbers in RDD sampling, which in turn reduces the time and cost of interviewing. If a reverse directory is unavailable, the information can also be estimated from regular telephone directories, but this is an extremely time-consuming task. It remains the decision of each surveyor whether or not to gather such information about each prefix. If, for example, "free" (i.e., no direct cost) student time is available to work on assembling such information but the researcher will have to pay for interviewers' time, then it may be well worth the effort to improve the efficiency of the sampling pool of telephone numbers by gathering such information.

If one intends to conduct RDD sampling of the same geographical area in several studies (i.e., year after year), then it is often worth the initial costs to gather as much information as possible about the prefixes in that area. Depending on residential mobility in the sampling area, it is important periodically to update both information about the proportion of households assigned to each prefix and information about ranges of nonoperating banks of suffixes.

Hand-Generated RDD Sampling Pools

Despite the computer being the clearly preferred approach to generating RDD sampling pools, it is instructive to begin by looking at the manual approach to producing a pool of telephone numbers to be used with RDD. This sequencing has been chosen because the manual approach is a methodical and simplified version of what the computer can do more quickly and efficiently, and so should be more easily understood by those readers new to this part of telephone survey methodology.

There are two techniques that can be used to generate RDD sampling pools by hand. First, one can use a random numbers table (found in the back of most statistics books) to choose strings of consecutive digits to serve as suffixes to add to three-digit prefixes that ring in the sampling area. Second, one can use the "add-a-digit" technique with telephone numbers sampled directly from telephone directories.

Using a random numbers table. The first example will illustrate the simplest case of RDD sampling pool generation, in which the only information known to the surveyor is the prefixes that ring in the sampling area. Once this list of prefixes has been assembled, one simply adds consecutive strings of four digits from the random numbers table to each prefix one at a time. Suppose one finds the following string of random digits: 547196353826. For the purposes of this example, suppose there were only three prefixes in the sampling area: 864, 866,

and 869. Then the first three telephone numbers generated would be
864-5471, 866-9635, and 869-3826. The person creating the sampling
pool would continue this process until a sufficient number of telephone
numbers had been generated. (How to estimate what is likely to be a
sufficiently large pool of telephone numbers is discussed later in this
chapter.)

If the surveyor also had complete and accurate information about the
relative proportion of telephone access lines within the sampling area
reached by each prefix, then it should be used so as to reduce interviewer
processing time and thus costs. With the above set of three prefixes,
suppose that 864 reached 20% of the households in the sampling area
and 866 and 869 each reached 40%. Then the person generating the
sampling pool from a random numbers table should add strings of four
digits to prefixes chosen in the following order: 864, 866, 866, 869, 869,
864, 866, 866, 869, 869, 864, and so on to reflect the relative distribution
of prefixes in the sampling area (i.e., 20:40:40). The advantage to this
approach is that it concentrates dialing those prefixes known to have a
greater likelihood of reaching a working telephone number, and it does
so *in proportion* to their relative frequency in the sampling area.

If accurate and complete information is also known about the ranges
of nonoperating (i.e., vacuous) banks of suffixes, this too can be used to
improve the efficiency of a sampling pool of RDD numbers in reaching
working telephones. Again, using the same set of three prefixes from the
above examples, assume the 864 prefix operates only with suffixes that
range from 2000 to 3999, the 866 prefix works for 5000-7999, and 869
works for 0000-0999 and 4000-4999. The person who is generating the
sampling pool should then choose strings of *only three digits* in length
from the random numbers table. Three random digits would then be
added to the following prefixes and the leading digit of each of the
suffixes known to be operating: 864-2, 864-3, 866-5, 866-6, 866-7, 869-0,
and 869-4. This process is what Sudman (1973) refers to as the "inverse
sampling method."

It should be noted that regardless of the method being used to
generate an RDD sample, information about prefixes is properly used
only when it is available for *all prefixes* in the sampling pool. In other
words, if the number of telephone access lines associated with a prefix is
known only for certain prefixes, this information must not be used in an
attempt to improve sampling efficiency because it may instead bias the
sampling process. The reason is that without such information about *all
prefixes* there will be no accurate way to calculate the relative
proportion of numbers that must be generated for each prefix. In those

cases it is best to leave it to interviewers' processing of numbers to allow for the proper sampling of prefixes to occur.

This "proper sampling" happens because of the self-weighting aspect of RDD surveys. That is, interviews will theoretically be completed at prefixes at a rate directly proportional to the relative frequency of those prefixes in the sampling area. When one has comparable information about *all prefixes* in the sampling area, the efficiency of this self-weighting process can be enhanced. If comparable information does not exist, the rule to follow is, "Let well enough alone!" This caveat also holds for information about vacuous banks of suffixes. Unless this information is known about all prefixes in the sampling area, it is best to employ the straightforward approach of simply using prefixes in equal proportions when generating the sampling pool.

An additional comment that holds for all RDD sampling: It is possible to combine the efficiency gained from knowing both the proportion of working numbers associated with each prefix and information about vacuous banks of suffixes associated with each prefix. This is rather complicated to do by hand, but it is possible, and if there are not too many prefixes it justifies the time and attentiveness it will demand.

The add-a-digit approach. Landon and Banks (1977) provide an empirical test of the efficiency of this general approach to generating telephone sampling pools. The add-a-digit technique samples "seed" numbers from a telephone directory, adds a digit (or two) to each seed, and uses these new numbers for sampling telephone access lines. The new numbers that are produced through this approach may be listed or unlisted.

The way in which digits are added can vary. For example, the "plus-one" approach can be used. In this case a number, such as 869-5025, is randomly or systematically chosen from a telephone directory that covers the sampling area. A 1 is added to the last digit of the suffix, producing the number 869-5026, which in turn enters the sampling pool. Another approach would be to add 11 or a one-digit or two-digit random number to each seed sampled from the directory.

The add-a-digit approach to sample generation is especially useful when one must quickly generate a relatively small sampling pool by hand; for example, one that might require upwards of 1000 telephone numbers. Add-a-digit also helps the survey process by shortening the interviewing period, as it increases the proportion of working numbers that will be dialed compared to simple RDD sampling. In two studies reported by Landon and Banks, the add-a-digit approach improved sampling efficiency by approximately 30%. Thus its effect is similar to the aforementioned technique in which information about nonoperating banks of suffixes is used to target the generation of telephone numbers within working banks of suffixes.

To use the add-a-digit approach one must first gather a comprehensive set of telephone directories and then determine the number of seeds that should be drawn from each book. In the simplest case there will be one directory. After estimating the size of the sampling pool that will be needed to achieve the desired sample size of completed interviews, the surveyor should compare this amount with the total number of telephone numbers listed in the directory or directories.

This is not difficult. Start by determining the number of pages in the telephone directory that will be used. (If more than one directory is used, this approach should be modified to accommodate possible different page sizes in different directories.) If, for example, there are 48 pages in a local directory, and if the size of the pool of telephone numbers that will be dialed is estimated at 800, then one would want to randomly or systematically choose 15 telephone numbers per page of the directory, then add a 1 to the last digit in each telephone number, thereby producing the set of telephone numbers that interviewers will actually dial.

Landon and Banks (1977) caution about possible bias in add-a-digit sampling that could result if telephone companies concentrate the assignment of unlisted telephone numbers to certain banks of suffixes. If this were to happen, the sample of telephone numbers based on the seeds listed in the directory might not have adequate external validity. In other words, the pool of numbers that were dialed may be biased against those who have unlisted telephone numbers. Despite this theoretical concern, I am unaware of any place where this is the practice followed by telephone companies in assigning unlisted numbers. Nevertheless, it is prudent that anyone planning to employ the add-a-digit approach first determine local telephone companies' policies.

Another technique similar to the add-a-digit method is simply to *replace* the last two digits of a seed number with two randomly sampled digits (Waksberg, 1978). For example, using a random numbers table, assume the digits 3 and 1 are the next two listed. If the number 475-5378 were picked from a telephone directory, then by replacing the last two digits (7 and 8) with the 3 and 1, a new number, 475-5331, would enter the sampling pool (not 475-5378). This approach has all the potential advantages and disadvantages of the add-a-digit approach, but because it is a more complicated and time-consuming technique, it is rarely the method of choice when generating an RDD sampling pool by hand.

If a surveyor plans to use a telephone survey on a one-shot basis (e.g., for a master's thesis) and is uncertain whether this method of data collection will be employed in the foreseeable future, then the manual approach to generating a pool of RDD numbers will probably be the preferred choice, provided the size of the pool is not extremely large (several thousand). In contrast, if the size of the pool of numbers that must be processed is very large or if a surveyor expects to be constantly using telephone surveys to gather data within the same sampling area, it is strongly recommended that RDD sampling pools be generated by computer.

Computer-Generated RDD Sampling Pools

Each of the techniques for generating RDD samples discussed above has its counterpart when using a computer to generate the sampling pool. When one has CATI, the steps taken to generate RDD samples are somewhat different than the realities facing persons without the system. With CATI, telephone numbers can be generated for use by interviewers *one at a time.* In addition, sampling pools need not be generated in advance; instead, when interviewers come to work the computer generates additional telephone numbers as needed. At present, however, most persons who would like to do telephone surveys do not have access to such systems. In contrast, persons without a CATI system will need to have a sufficiently large sampling pool of RDD numbers waiting for interviewers *in advance* of interviewing sessions, as it would be impractical to have someone at interviewing sessions generating RDD numbers one-at-a-time as interviewers needed them.

As with all RDD sampling pool generation, the use of a computer begins with the collection of an exhaustive list of all prefixes that ring within the sampling boundaries. As previously discussed, it can be quite cost-effective to gather additional information about each prefix: specifically, (1) the number of residential accounts associated with each prefix and (2) ranges of vacuous suffix banks for each prefix. A reminder: Unless additional information is available for *all prefixes* used in sampling, it should not be used!

Thus with the possibility of three types of prefix information available, there are four situations a surveyor will encounter:

(1) having the list of prefixes only;
(2) having the list of prefixes and information about the number of accounts on each prefix;
(3) having the list of prefixes and ranges of vacuous suffixes for each prefix; and
(4) having all three types of information.

(The computer routine listed in Appendix A can be adapted to each of these situations, but in its printed form assumes that all three types of information are available.)

Prefixes only. The simplest case occurs when the surveyor has only the list of prefixes that ring in the sampling area. In this instance a computer is programmed to assign an equal number of random suffixes to each prefix until a sufficiently large pool of numbers has been generated. If, for example, one has an estimated need for a sampling pool with 1,000 RDD numbers and there are 10 prefixes in the sampling area, then simple division suggests that each prefix should be paired with 100 unique strings of four-digit random numbers. The following BASIC program, for example, would run on an IBM-PC and would generate and print 1,000 numbers, 100 for each of the 10 prefixes listed in the DATA statements:

```
  5 RANDOMIZE TIMER
 10 FOR I=1 TO 10
 20    READ PREFIX(I)
 30    FOR X=1 TO 100
 40      SUFF1=INT(RND*9)
 50      SUFF2=INT(RND*9)
 60      SUFF3=INT(RND*9)
 70      SUFF4=INT(RND*9)
 80      LPRINT PREFIX(I);"-";SUFF1;SUFF2;SUFF3;SUFF4
 90    NEXT X
100 NEXT I
110 DATA 251,256,328,475,491,492,570,864,866,869
```

With use of a computer (or even a random numbers table) to generate random digit strings there is a small probability that duplicate strings will be generated and matched with the same prefix. In other words, if the string 4567 were generated and matched with two different prefixes (e.g., 866-4567 and 869-4567), there would be no problem. But occasionally exactly the same telephone number will appear again, by chance. In the case of hand-generated samples, it could be impractical to check for duplicates. However, computers can easily check for duplicates, and it is worth incorporating such a routine into the program.

In addition to cleaning the sampling pool for duplicates, one may choose to program the computer to perform other "cleaning" procedures, such as eliminating all numbers that end in 00 and/or 000 and/or 0000. These numbers are often nonresidential; thus eliminating them can save on interviewer processing time without necessarily compromising the validity of the sampling pool. This should be done with caution and only after checking a reverse directory to determine the validity of this assumption. Because businesses, by their very nature, list their telephone numbers, a fairly quick check of a reverse directory will indicate whether telephone numbers that end in multiple zeros are almost all business numbers. If this is not the case, then such a cleaning routine should not be used.

Nonworking banks of suffixes. When banks of nonoperating suffixes have been identified, this information can also be incorporated into the computer routine. This can be done in two ways. First as mentioned earlier, if banks of suffixes in ranges of 1,000 can be identified as nonoperating (e.g., 1000-1999 or 3000-3999), then the computer can be programmed to utilize such information at the beginning of its routine.

A second approach is to have four-digit numbers (i.e., the three digits of the prefix and the leading digit of the suffix) read in as data and program the computer to generate random strings of *three* digits in length. Using an earlier example, suppose there are three prefixes in the sampling area and each has a relatively narrow range of operating suffixes: 864-2000 through 864-3999, 866-5000 through 866-7999, 869-0000 through 869-0999, and 869-4000 through 869-4999. In this case the following four-digit strings should be read as data: 8642, 8643, 8665, 8666, 8667, 8690, and 8694. The the computer would be programmed to add strings of three random digits. This would generate a pool of RDD numbers concentrated only in those banks of suffixes known to contain working telephones.

Number of access lines. Finally, if a surveyor knows the number of telephone access lines associated with each prefix, the sampling pool of

RDD numbers can be stratified by prefix. Again, for the sake of simplicity let us assume that information about vacuous suffixes is not known. If it were determined that the 864 prefix had 4,000 working numbers, 866 had 3,000, and 869 had 1,000, one would first start by calculating the relative frequency (proportion) of each prefix in the sampling area. Here, of the 8,000 total access lines 50% are reached via 864, 37.5% via 866, and 12.5% via 869. Thus if a researcher estimated that interviewers would need to process 1,000 RDD numbers, then the sampling pool should contain 500 with the 864 prefix, 375 with 866 and 125 with 869.

To accomplish this with an IBM-PC, for example, the BASIC program presented earlier would be modified as follows:

```
  5 RANDOMIZE TIMER
 10 FOR I=1 TO 3
 20    READ PREFIX(I)
 25    READ NUMB(J)
 30    FOR X=1 TO NUMB(J)
 40       SUFF1=INT(RND*9)
 50       SUFF2=INT(RND*9)
 60       SUFF3=INT(RND*9)
 70       SUFF4=INT(RND*9)
 80       LPRINT PREFIX(I);"-";SUFF1;SUFF2;SUFF3;SUFF4
 90    NEXT X
100 NEXT I
110 DATA 864, 500, 866, 375, 869, 125
```

If information also was known about vacuous suffix banks for each prefix, it too could be incorporated into the program, though, as before, adjustments would need to be programmed into the routine to reflect the proper proportion of the final sampling pool associated with each prefix.

DIRECTORY AND
LIST-BASED SAMPLING POOLS

In many instances random-digit dialing is unnecessary to meet the surveyor's needs, and this will usually depend on the purpose of the survey. The reader is reminded that RDD surveying is the best method to select a representative sample of households (with telephones) from the general population. But when an exhaustive listing of the population of interest is available, then sampling can and usually should be done from this listing.

An example of list sampling would be a telephone survey of members of a professional organization (e.g., retired military officers), in which the organization has a complete listing of each member's home and/or business telephone number. Another example of list sampling would be a telephone survey of students currently enrolled at a college or university, in which a list from the registrar's office would define the entire population of interest. As mentioned before, in rural areas of the United States few persons appear to have unlisted telephone numbers, and there often is a very low rate of population ingress. In areas such as this the local telephone directory can be used to pick numbers for the sampling pool.

Forming a sampling pool via list sampling is uncomplicated and can be done *randomly* or *systematically*. The random approach, however, is rarely necessary provided one samples in a systematic fashion throughout the entire listing. Yet some persons may still prefer to choose the random approach, and thus a brief illustration is appropriate.

An example of the random approach. Suppose that a telephone survey of 200 elementary school teachers' satisfaction with working conditions was to be conducted by a local school district that employed 1,800 teachers. In the easiest case the district's computer could be programmed to choose 200 names randomly for the sampling pool. (The reader is reminded that in almost all telephone surveys the sampling pool will need to be larger than the final sample size desired. But for this example we will assume that all teachers who are picked for the sampling pool will be reached and will participate in the survey.) If there was no computer to generate this sample, it could be done by hand in a variety of ways using a random numbers table. One way would be to use two-digit strings of random numbers to count forward to the next name on a complete alphabetical listing of all 1,800 teachers. For example, if the random numbers table showed the string, 0417565432, then the fourth teacher on an alphabetical listing would be the first one to enter the sampling pool. Next, the person generating the sample would count ahead 17 names to choose the second teacher, then ahead 56 names for the third, and so on. Using this approach to sampling 200 names from the listing of 1,800 would require the person doing the sampling to go back through the list approximately five to six times on average. This follows from the fact that, by chance, one pass through the list would sample approximately 36 names, which in turn projects the need to go through the list about 5.5 times to get the 200 names needed for the desired sample.

The systematic approach. A much easier and equally as valid approach is a systematic sampling from a list. Take the same example in which the school district wanted to interview 200 teachers via telephone from a staff of 1,800; thus, one-ninth of the staff should be sampled. First, choose a random number from 1 through 9 and count that many names from the start of the alphabetical listing to sample the first teacher. After that, simply choose every ninth name on the list. If the random start is the number 2, then the second teacher on the list would be the first name to enter the list. After that the sample would include the 11th, 20th, 29th, 38th, and so on name on the list.

When sampling from a very long list, such as a local telephone book, it is much easier not to count ahead to names, one at a time. The following example illustrates a technique that accomplishes the same systematic sampling more quickly. Assume that a sampling pool of 300 residential telephone numbers was to be drawn from a directory. Also assume the directory had 50 pages, with four columns of numbers on each page; thus one should sample six numbers per page (300/50 = 6). Because there are four columns per page, one could choose some arbitrary (i.e., unbiased) scheme for sampling within columns. The possibilities are many. For illustration, however, one could sample the tenth residential listing from the top in each of the four columns and the fifth from the bottom in the first two columns, thus yielding a total of six names per page.

The important thing to remember with list sampling is to employ a technique that chooses names *across the entire* listing. Because lists are typically alphabetized, this results in choosing a representative sample of names throughout the alphabet. Similarly, if a list is ordered by seniority (i.e., those with longest membership come first on the list), then by sampling across the entirety of the listing a representative sample will be generated that is uncorrelated with length of membership.

Reverse directories can also be used to sample persons within small, localized geographic areas, such as neighborhoods where RDD sampling would prove much too costly. As long as the purpose of the survey does not necessitate true random sampling, then systematic list sampling will often be valid. To determine the number of households to sample per block, it is best to use a detailed street map. If the map shows actual housing units, then proportional sampling can be done to represent the approximate population per block in the final sample. If this level of information is not readily available, a surveyor may simply count the number of block faces in the geographic sampling area and divide the desired size of the sampling pool by this amount. The quotient would then be used as the number of telephone numbers to sample per block. For example, suppose an evaluation researcher had a control neighborhood and a treatment neighborhood in which 500 telephone numbers would be needed to complete 300 interviews in each neighborhood. If each neighborhood had approximately 100 block faces, then five telephone numbers should be drawn in a random or systematic fashion from each block (this approach assumes that the population and/or the number of households per block face is approximately equal). Finally, the proper use of a reverse directory also requires that accurate information be available about the starting and ending address number on each block; thus the advantage provided by a detailed street-level map. (These maps are often available from city governments' planning departments.)

At present many organizations have computerized their employee or membership lists. In such cases their computer software may be capable of drawing a random or systematic sample from the entire listing. As computer technology continues its saturation of society, more and more of the software that controls listings should be flexible enough to begin to eliminate the need to draw sampling pools from lists by hand. In addition, it is likely that reverse directories will also become readily available for use on minis and micros either on diskettes, on tape, or via downloading.

HOW LARGE A SAMPLING POOL
SHOULD BE GENERATED?

In an ideal telephone survey every number dialed would be working, every selected respondent would be available for the interview at the time of the call, and no respondent would refuse. Of course, nothing even remotely approaching this ideal ever happens with surveys. Every sample of telephone numbers, even the most up-to-date list samples, will reach nonworking numbers. Some small proportion of designated respondents are likely never to be available during the survey's field period. Finally, it is highly unlikely that the refusal rate for telephone surveys can be kept near zero (or even below 10%, for that matter).

The result of this attrition often requires a sampling pool that is *far larger* than the number of completed interviews desired by the surveyor. It is the surveyor's responsibility to choose a final sample size that is large enough to support the survey's purpose, but it is not the purpose of this text to advise the reader fully on how to make this decision. Other texts that deal with margin of error and statistical power should be consulted if the reader is unfamiliar with this decision-making process. For example, Sudman (1976) has an entire chapter ("How Big Should the Sample Be?") for those persons planning surveys designed to estimate some univariate population parameter. (As used by Sudman, the word "sample" refers to the number of completed interviews, not the size of the sampling pool that will be processed to achieve the completions.) For those whose survey is designed to measure bivariate and/or multivariate interrelationships, the notion of statistical power and sample size is addressed by Hays (1973) and Cohen and Cohen (1982).

For review, the reader is reminded that when a survey is designed to estimate the level at which some variable exists within a given population and probability sampling is employed, the degree of precision of the survey's estimates will be enhanced as the sample size increases. In the case of a binomial variable (e.g., a survey item that has a "Yes" or "No" response) with a heterogeneous (50-50) split and with simple random sampling, a sample size of 100 will have a margin of error of approximately plus or minus 10 percentage points, at the 95 percent confidence interval. For a sample of 1,000 this precision improves to approximately plus or minus three percentage points. With sample sizes approaching 10,000 it reduces to about plus or minus one percentage point. All these figures presume that sampling is done from some arbitrarily large (i.e., infinite) population. If the size of the population being sampled is relatively small (i.e., 10,000 or less), the margin of error for a particular sample size begins to decrease as the finite size of the population itself decreases.

As mentioned before, those with a CATI system may be able to avoid the need to generate the sampling pool before starting the survey. Without CATI, however, one must generate a sufficiently large sampling pool for the entire survey *before* interviewing begins; or at a minimum, one must have enough numbers on hand to get through the first interviewing session and then generate more numbers prior to the start of each subsequent session. Because it can be quite inconvenient to generate new numbers day after day, it is strongly recommended to those without CATI that the entire sampling pool be generated before interviewing begins but that numbers be released from the pool for processing by interviewers on a daily basis and in a tightly controlled fashion (as discussed in Chapters 3 and 6).

If this approach is followed, one must know how to estimate an adequate-sized sampling pool. The practical objective is to produce enough numbers in advance so that one need not do this a second, third, or fourth time or more. On the other hand, it is not cost-effective to generate an unnecessarily immense sampling pool, even when using a computer. To produce a realistic estimate of how many numbers are likely to be needed in a particular survey, one must answer the following questions:

(1) What size final sample is desired?
(2) What is the likely "hit rate" for working numbers?
(3) What proportion of working numbers will be screened out due to specific respondent exclusion criteria?
(4) What proportion of eligible respondents will be lost to the final sample due to refusals or because they were never available during the survey's field period?

This information can then be used in the following formula to estimate the size of the sampling pool:

ESTIMATED SIZE OF SAMPLING POOL = (FSS)/((HR)(1-REC)(1-LE))

FSS

The final sample size (FSS) is the number of completed interviews the surveyor has determined is needed for the purposes of the survey. As mentioned earlier, this is an extremely important decision, based in part on the availability of resources to support data collection.

HR

The hit rate (HR) is an estimation of the proportion of telephone numbers in the sampling pool that are likely to be working and will ring at appropriate locations (e.g., residences, not businesses). The hit rate will vary across sampling areas. The most accurate way to estimate HR is to gather comprehensive information from local telephone companies or local directories. For example, with a reverse directory, one can estimate the density of working numbers for each prefix in the sampling area. Here some knowledge of the proportion of numbers that are likely to be unlisted is also useful.

The experience of others can also provide one with safe estimates for the HR value. Groves and Kahn (1979) found in their national RDD samples that approximately 20% of the numbers in their sampling pool reached residences. In this case the value of HR would be .20. In my own experience with localized samples throughout the Midwest and East, the HR value often ranges from .30 to .50. For example, in the metropolitan Chicago area (the 312 area code) most prefixes are very densely packed with working numbers; thus it is not unusual for a prefix to have been assigned to 4,000-6,000 residences out of a possible 10,000. As one moves farther from a central city, though, the HR value is likely to decrease, so it is best to gather information to make an estimate with each new sampling area.

Something else to keep in mind when estimating the HR value is the proportion of numbers likely to be nonresidential. Currently there is about a 3:1 ratio of residential to nonresidential telephone access lines in the United States.

REC

Any respondent exclusion criteria (REC) that make certain persons or households *ineligible* will increase the size of the sampling pool. This value, which represents the proportion of households that will be lost due to selection criteria, is fairly easy to calculate but often requires recent census information for the sampling area. If, for example, only males over the age of 17 years can be interviewed, then approximately one-third of all households will be lost because persons fitting this demographic requirement will not live there. In this case the REC value would be .33.

In many metropolitan areas a survey that had to screen for senior citizens (over the age of 59 years) would find that more than four out of every five residences reached via RDD would not have such a person living there. In this case REC might be as high as .80 or .85.

RDD surveys designed to sample respondents within the boundaries of particular communities often have to employ geographic screeneis. In these cases the surveyor must be able to estimate the REC value for those that will be reached by RDD but lost because they live outside the sampling area.

Fortunately, many surveys will not be targeted to some specialized segment of the general population, other than those persons over the age of 17 years (i.e., adults). As such, the effective REC for many surveys is at or near zero (.00). But as eligibility criteria become more restricted, this value can grow and may eventually rule against the use of a survey that samples telephone numbers from the general population. (For many varied practical reasons, I use .10-.20 as the REC range below which I advise those contemplating telephone surveys to reconsider seriously other approaches to sampling.)

LE

The loss of eligibles (LE) is the final factor one must consider when estimating the size of the sampling pool. Even with the best group of well-supervised and experienced telephone interviewers, the LE value is likely to range from .15 to .25 largely because of refusals. Experience shows that as sampling of the general population is concentrated more and more in central cities, and especially as the quality of interviewing decreases, LE can reach or even exceed .50. In this case one must question the validity of conducting the survey in the first place. (The issue of how to minimize the LE value is discussed in Chapters 5 and 6.)

An Example of Estimating the Size
of the Sampling Pool

In a survey that was planned as this chapter was written, a client of the Northwestern University Survey Laboratory wanted 300 interviews completed in the city of Chicago via RDD with white or black males of non-Jewish and non-Arabic descent, 25 years of age or older. For this survey FSS equaled 300. The HR value for the city of Chicago is aproximately .50. Based on the respondent screening that would be needed once a residence has been contacted, REC was about .50. Finally, with this exclusively male sample in the city of Chicago, the effective LE was estimated at about .40.

Using the formula,

ESTIMATED SIZE OF SAMPLING POOL = $(300)/((.50)(1-.50)(1-.4)) = 2000$

for this survey it was estimated that upwards of 2,000 telephone numbers would be needed for processing by interviewers in the course of completing the 300 interviews. To be on the safe side, my own preference is to inflate this estimate further about 10%. Thus in this example a sampling pool of 2,200 numbers was advised.

EXERCISES

1. Generate a sampling pool (manually) of 20 telephone numbers using a random numbers table. Use the following set of prefixes in equal proportions: 328-, 475-, 491-, and 866-.

2. Generate a sampling pool (manually) of 100 telephone numbers using a random numbers table. Use the following prefixes and leading suffix-digits; also stratify the sampling pool by prefix using the proportions shown in parentheses: 328-1 (10%), 328-3 (20%), 475-6 (6%), 475-7 (5%), 475-8 (4%), 475-9 (10%), 491-2 (22%), 866-0 (15%), and 866-1 (8%).

3. For those with access to and knowledge of SPSS, use the information from Exercise 2 in steps 1, 2 and 3 of the program in Appendix A.

4. Estimate the prevalence of unpublished telephone numbers in a local municipality. Use the local telephone directory for that municipality and the most recent census data on the number of households in the municipality.

5. Calculate the estimated size of a sampling pool that should be generated for the following survey using the local municipality in Exercise 4. In the survey 500 interviews will be completed with one adult, 40 years of age or older, per household. Assume that one in every four eligible respondents will refuse to participate and that one in every 15 of the other eligible respondents will never be reached to complete the interview during the time the survey is being conducted.

3

PROCESSING SAMPLING POOLS

The manner in which the sampling pool is processed will greatly determine the representativeness of the survey's final sample. There are several recommended approaches to instituting a system to control the processing of the telephone numbers in the sampling pool. This chapter focuses on the use of a "call-sheet" for each telephone number in the sampling pool, on which interviewers record the disposition (outcome) of each attempted dialing. It is through the use of the call-sheet that supervisory personnel control the processing of the sampling pool.

Chapter 2 explained how sampling pools for telephone surveys are produced; this chapter discusses the controlled use of the telephone numbers in the sampling pool. The primary goal of controlling the processing of telephone survey sampling pools is to finish the survey with as representative a sample of completed interviews as possible. The major advantage of telephone surveys as opposed to other survey methods is the centralized control it affords over the entire sampling and interviewing process. The care with which the sampling pool is processed by interviewers and supervisory personnel is a critical facet of this control of quality.

Chapter 3 begins with an overview of why and how sampling pools are controlled. The use of a call-sheet is then explained. A call-sheet is a form that is assigned to each number released from the sampling pool. Included in this section is a detailed discussion of various outcomes (dispositions) that may occur when interviewers dial telephone numbers and an explanation of how interviewers should handle different dispositions. It is these individual outcomes that are used by supervisory personnel to determine whether (and when) to have interviewers redial a telephone number. The following section provides some perspective on the pattern of dispositions that may be expected when processing sampling pools. Chapter 3 concludes with a discussion of how the processing of sampling pools is related to the various response rates associated with telephone surveys.

ISSUES IN CONTROLLING
THE SAMPLING POOL

The primary reason for having a formal system to control the use of numbers released from the sampling pool is to avoid the bias that could result if interviewers were allowed simply to choose telephone numbers from the sampling pool at whim. For example, only through use of a highly routinized system will hard-to-reach respondents get called back a sufficient number of times. If this is not done, the final sample will be disproportionately filled with easy-to-reach respondents. Because hard-to-reach respondents in a survey of the general population are most likely to be younger and male and easy-to-reach respondents are more likely to be older and female, the external validity (generalizability) of the final sample would be compromised. To avoid this problem a surveyor must employ a formal system of control over the numbers that are dialed by interviewers.

A formal system of control also improves interviewer efficiency by removing the responsibility for scheduling call-backs from interviewers. In turn this permits interviewers to concentrate on doing their best possible interviewing, as opposed to also being concerned with determining which numbers should be processed. Furthermore, if efforts are made to "convert" initial refusals (i.e., calling back to persuade persons who initially refused to participate to complete the interview), these call-sheets can be individually rescheduled at times deemed best by the person who is controlling the sampling pool.

In sum, by having supervisory personnel retain total responsibility for providing interviewers with numbers from the sampling pool, any bias that could enter the final sample if interviewers chose numbers for themselves is more likely to be avoided.

When a telephone survey is conducted without a CATI system, the control and sorting of processed telephone numbers from the sampling pool is done manually through a paper-and-pencil system. This paper-and-pencil approach is addressed in detail in this chapter. With the manual approach, there are three basic steps to controlling a sampling pool:

Step 1: Interviewers should be given a relatively small group of telephone numbers with which to start the interviewing session.

Step 2: A supervisor will need to provide additional numbers to interviewers during the interviewing session.

Step 3: Before the next interviewing session begins the group of numbers that were processed during the previous session must be sorted.

Experience strongly recommends that *one person* be given complete responsibility for this final step.

The preferred way for this level of control to be instituted is through the use of a separate call-sheet (as shown in Figure 2) that is assigned to each telephone number released from the sampling pool. By having a unique call-sheet for each telephone number dialed by interviewers, a "history" (or call record) can be constructed that explains what happened each time a particular telephone number is dialed.

The reader should note that the approaches to controlling the sampling pool described in this chapter are partly a matter of personal choice. I have successfully employed these paper-and-pencil, hand-sorted systems for nearly 10 years. Most other survey organizations without CATI use similar systems, but not always with such a detailed set of disposition codes or with as much demanding follow-through (i.e., reprocessing) of individual telephone numbers.

The approaches presented here are not the only valid systems that can be employed. After reading this chapter one could choose to devise a modified system to best meet his or her own needs. The important point remains: Without CATI, quality telephone surveys necessitate a constant and attentive human control of the processing of telephone numbers released from the sampling pool.

USING THE CALL-SHEET TO CONTROL
THE SAMPLING POOL

As mentioned above, every telephone number released from the sampling pool is printed on a separate piece of paper, the call-sheet, on which interviewers record information that allows supervisory personnel subsequently to decide what to do with each number that has been processed. Some organizations refer to this sheet as the "call record"; others designate it the "interviewer report form."

To be certain of the meaning of the phrase, "released from the sampling pool," the reader is reminded that it is not necessary to process all numbers that were generated in the sampling pool. As discussed in Chapter 2, without a CATI system it is recommended that the entire sampling pool be generated in advance of interviewing. Telephone numbers from the sampling pool are then released to interviewers *only as needed*. To maximize the external validity of the final sample, all numbers that are released from the pool should be fully processed (i.e., called back the proper number of times), but no threat to validity results when one does not need to release all the numbers originally generated to reach the desired number of completions.

Figure 2 is an example of the basic call-sheet used at the Northwestern University Survey Laboratory. It is modeled after the form used by the Survey Research Laboratory at the University of Illinois and is similar to that used by many other survey organizations. Its purpose is to provide interviewers with a formalized structure to record important information about every dialing of each telephone number that is released from the sampling pool.

The information to be written on the call-sheet shown in Figure 2 includes the date, time, and disposition of each dialing. The *disposition* refers to the coded outcome of each dialing (e.g., ring-no-answer, busy, out-of-order, refusal, completed, call-back, etc.). The interviewer is also expected to record her or his ID number with each dialing. Finally, the form provides space for annotation that can be extremely helpful both to the person who sorts processed call-sheets and to other interviewers who may subsequently redial the telephone number.

As will be discussed in Chapter 4, these call-sheets are typically paired with another sheet that contains the introductory spiel for the survey and the respondent selection procedure. Call-sheets are attached to a questionnaire only after an interview has been completed. As shown in Figure 2, the telephone number is printed in the upper left corner. Note that space is provided toward the upper right so that a unique questionnaire number (a respondent ID number) can be assigned later. Call-sheets for different surveys should be printed with different titles (and possibly on different colored paper), especially when an organization or a group of interviewers is conducting two or more surveys simultaneously.

Prior to the actual dialing of a telephone number, an interviewer should record the date and time in the appropriate columns across the next open row of call attempts. The date need only be the month and day (e.g., 05/09 should be recorded for the ninth of May). Interviewers should have their own watches, or, better yet, a wall clock should be positioned in a centralized location easily seen by all interviewers. Finally, before placing the call the interviewer should also record his or her ID; in most cases this will be a two-digit identification, but with small groups of interviewers initials are acceptable.

```
                    ------ User Supplied Title ------
Telephone Number
                                    Questionnaire #: __ __ __ __
   ###-####
---------------------------------------------------------------
Contact                             Disposition   Interviewer
Attempts    Date        Time           Code          I.D.
---------------------------------------------------------------

   1        __/__       __:__         ___ ___      ___ ___

   2        __/__       __:__         ___ ___      ___ ___

   3        __/__       __:__         ___ ___      ___ ___

   4        __/__       __:__         ___ ___      ___ ___

   5        __/__       __:__         ___ ___      ___ ___

   6        __/__       __:__         ___ ___      ___ ___

                           NOTES
   1.  _____
   2.  _____
   3.  _____
   4.  _____
   5.  _____
   6.  _____
```

Figure 2. Example of a Call-Sheet

It is important that interviewers record the date and time the call was placed so that telephone numbers that need to be redialed can be scheduled appropriately. Because call attempts are spaced throughout the period in which the survey is being fielded (conducted), having the date and time recorded allows supervisory personnel to determine best when to reprocess a number. In some cases, especially with numbers that consistently ring without answer, the person who is responsible for controlling the sampling pool must hold aside a call-sheet for a particular day and time.

Accountability is the primary reason for having interviewers record their ID number. This allows supervisory personnel to determine which interviewer placed a particular call. Knowing such information is critical to the successful resolution of problems that will inevitably arise; it also provides the means whereby an interviewer's productivity can be estimated. Apart from all this, the psychology underlying such a system reinforces the notion that high-quality work is expected from individual interviewers and that this productivity is constantly monitored.

The most crucial information that is recorded on the call-sheet is the disposition code, indicating the outcome of each dialing. It is through inspection of the disposition code that call-sheets can be quickly and efficiently sorted after each interviewing session. The set of disposition categories and their associated numerical codes that are described in the following pages are fairly exhaustive and can easily be collapsed into broader categories if a surveyor so chooses. The important point is that for most telephone surveys some numerical coding scheme should be used by interviewers in order to enhance the ability of supervisory personnel to control the sampling pool. Use of such a formal system also serves to reinforce the professionalism that should be expected of interviewers.

Figure 3 presents one such coding scheme. The reader should note that the numerical codes that are assigned to different dispositions are arbitrary; that is, there is nothing special about the particular numbering used in Figure 3.

The set of dispositions listed in Figure 3 is fairly typical for surveys of the general population that employ a formal respondent selection procedure *within* each household that is contacted. A set of codes such as this should be used regardless of whether the sampling pool was generated from a directory or listing or via some RDD method. Depending on the particular purpose of the survey, the surveyor may need to institute other disposition codes. For example, when a panel survey is being conducted (i.e., one in which the same respondents are reinterviewed after some passage of time, such as one year later), disposition codes are needed for the different reasons that a person can no longer be reached via the telephone number at which he or she had been reached during the previous wave of the panel.

For the purposes of the following explanation of the dispositions shown in Figure 3, I will refer to the supervisory person responsible for controlling the overall processing of telephone numbers as the sampling pool's *controller*. As mentioned above, I recommend that one person be charged with this responsibility; which includes determining when to

Disposition Code	Explanation
10	No answer after seven rings
11	Busy, after one immediate redial
12	Answering machine (residence)
13	Household language barrier
14	Answered by nonresident
15	Household refusal; use 15H for immediate hang-up without comment
20	Disconnected or other nonworking
21	Temporarily disconnected
22	Business, other nonresidence
23	No one meets eligibility criteria
30	Contact only
31	Selected respondent temporarily unavailable
32	Selected respondent unavailable during field period
33	Selected respondent unavailable due to physical/ mental handicap
34	Language barrier with selected respondent
35	Refusal by selected respondent
36	Partial interview; use 36R for refusal
37	Completed interview

Figure 3. Example of Disposition Codes for Controlling a Sampling Pool

release particular call-sheets to interviewers, when to reschedule the processing of a call-sheet, and when to remove a call-sheet from further processing. This latter decision will depend in part on how many call-backs interviewers are expected to make with ring-no-answers and hard-to-reach respondents.

Ring-No-Answer

In the majority of times that interviewers dial a telephone number, especially with RDD sampling, they will not complete an interview. In many of these cases they will not reach anyone at all—the telephone will ring without being answered. Several RDD surveys we have conducted in the past 10 years show that upwards of four out of every 10 dialings made by interviewers result in the number ringing but not being answered.

As shown in Figure 3, a disposition code representing the ring-no-answer outcome is assigned by interviewers after a predetermined number of rings have elapsed without the telephone being answered. The number of rings interviewers should allow before hanging up depends on the surveyor's preference. On the low side, probably no fewer than five rings should occur before an interviewer hangs up. On the high end, it is likely to be a waste of person time if interviewers allow telephones to ring more than 10 times. An exception to this would be for telephone numbers that have been dialed on several previous occasions without ever being answered. In this case it is wise to have interviewers allow the telephone to ring in excess of 10 times before hanging up. At the Northwestern University Survey Laboratory a middle ground is taken; interviewers are expected to allow a telephone to ring seven times before coding it a ring-no-answer.

Ring-no-answers are normally reprocessed once per session, session after session, until a predetermined number of call-backs has been made. How many call-backs should be made is based in part on the resources available to support the survey and on the length of the field period. In terms of telephone numbers that ring and yet are never answered, and depending on the specifics of the survey, one can expect as much as 5% of a sampling pool to fall into this category, even after as many as five call-backs (Skogan, 1978).

Busy Signals

In most cases a busy signal is a good sign because it usually means that someone can eventually be reached at the number. Busy signals should be coded as busy after the interviewer has immediately redialed the number. The reason to have interviewers immediately redial busy numbers is to make certain they dialed correctly the first time, and also to take advantage of the small possibility that whoever was using the telephone at the time of the first dialing was in the process of finishing the conversation.

At the surveyor's discretion, interviewers can be permitted to redial busy numbers later in an interviewing session. If this practice is followed, there must be a limit on how often the interviewer can call back, otherwise the disposition code column of the call-sheet will get quickly filled up with "busys." I believe it is reasonable to have interviewers redial busy numbers one or two more times in a session, but only after delays of at least 15 minutes.

A minor problem that should be guarded against is misidentifying the "fast busy" signal. This is a tone used by some telephone companies to indicate a nonworking number. If interviewers are alerted to these signals, they are less likely to confuse them with normal busy signals and thereby will conserve the time that would otherwise be wasted on unnecessary redialings. A fast busy signal should be coded as a nonworking number, not normal busy, so the controller will remove the call-sheet from further processing.

Answering Machines

As the cost of answering machines continues to drop, more of the general public will come to use them. If an answering machine indicates that a business has been reached and the survey is one of residences, then the disposition code for nonresidence should be used, rather than the disposition code for an answering machine (see Figure 3). For times when the interviewer is uncertain of who has been reached, or suspects that it may be a residence, answering machines deserve their own unique disposition codes because this informs the controller that an interview may eventually be completed at this number.

A decision faced with answering machines is whether or not to have the interviewer leave a message. My recommendation is to have interviewers do so in order to personalize the contact, but the message should be brief, polite, and *standardized*. In other words, all interviewers should be instructed precisely what to say when they reach a residential answering machine. The message should be similar to the introduction that is used in the survey: It should identify the survey organization or group, and the purpose and importance of the survey, and it should inform the resident that a call-back will be made.

The controller must give special attention to those numbers that reach answering machines. By looking at patterns of call attempts and dispositions on the call-sheet, a telephone number that has consistently reached an answering machine can be held aside for recycling on certain days or at certain times that have not been tried before. This will depend partly on the length of the survey's field period.

Household Language Barrier

The closer a survey's sampling area is to a central city, the more often interviewers will reach households whose telephones are answered by persons who do not speak English, or at least cannot speak it well enough to communicate with the interviewer. Nowadays this happens with new immigrants, especially those of Asian or Hispanic descent, and with older European immigrants who still prefer to speak their native country's language.

There is some reason to believe that on certain occasions "no English" (or "no hablo Ingles," for example) is used as a ploy to avoid speaking to the interviewer. When this occurs it really constitutes a refusal if the person can speak English better than he or she admits. Unfortunately, there is no standardized way for an interviewer to determine if this is happening.

When language appears to be a barrier, interviewers should code it as such without arguing with the person with whom they are speaking, even if they suspect the person's veracity. If resources allow, the controller should recycle these numbers during another interviewing session, taking the chance that on the second dialing a person who can and will communicate in English will answer. This can be especially useful in surveys that utilize a systematic *within*-household selection procedure (as discussed in Chapter 4), as the person ultimately selected as the respondent may in fact be able to speak English.

For surveys that employ Spanish lanauage interviewers in addition to those who speak English, our experience with Chicago's fairly large and somewhat undocumented (illegal) Hispanic population is that more than half of all interviews conducted with persons who identify themselves as Hispanic can be done in English. Thus the problem of missing non-English-speaking households in the general population is often relatively small, even when a survey cannot afford non-English interviewing. (Non-English interviewing requires that the questionnaire be translated and printed in a second language. Interviewers who are bilingual cannot "interpret" questions on their own. If this was done, all standardization of question form would be lost because respondents would no longer hear exactly the same wording.)

Answered by Nonresident

On rare occasions a telephone is answered by someone who does not live at the household and the interviewer is told that none of the occupants are at home. This happens with babysitters, housesitters, cleaning persons, and friends or relatives who have dropped in to check while occupants are away on vacation. In such instances interviewers should explain the reason they are calling and try to determine when a resident will be home. This information should be written in the notes section of the call-sheet. The controller can then have an interviewer reprocess the number on the appropriate day.

Household Refusals

Most refusals of telephone surveys occur shortly after the telephone has been answered and before a designated respondent has been selected from within the household. Thus they are coded as *household* refusals. In all cases interviewers should write an explanation of the nature of the refusal on the call-sheet.

Persons often say, "we don't have time," "we don't do surveys," "we're not interested," "we don't give out that type of information," and sometimes merely hang up without response. In this latter instance some proportion of no-comment hangups may be at non-English households. Therefore, interviewers should be instructed to code such outcomes with a separate disposition code (as shown in Figure 3), indicating that it may possibly be a non-English household. This allows the controller to recycle these call-sheets with bilingual interviewers, if such interviewers are available.

From the standpoint of processing the sample, the surveyor should make an a priori decision about attempts to convert refusals. From experience, it appears that regardless of what people give as their reason for refusing, in the majority of cases it seems that the timing of the call was not right. An interviewer may have reached the household at an inconvenient time, or the person answering the telephone may simply have been in a bad mood.

As discussed in Chapter 5, interviewers must be trained to be politely persistent when someone refuses before giving up on that particular call attempt. Once an interviewer senses that a particular dialing will result in a refusal, however, he or she should terminate the exchange by commenting along the following lines: "OK, I'm sorry we bothered you at this time."

For surveys with lengthy field periods (two or more weeks), many survey organizations have a standard practice of recycling household refusals a second time, on the chance that the telephone will be answered by someone willing to cooperate. When this is done the controller should let a few days pass before the call-sheet is reintroduced. In other cases "hard-core" refusals may be routed to interviewers with a special knack of eliciting cooperation. Whatever decision is followed, household refusals merit special attention as the sampling pool is being processed because too high a refusal rate can threaten the external validity of the final sample.

Nonworking Numbers

The practices of the telephone companies operating within the sampling area determine the ease with which nonworking numbers are identified. Closer to central cities, most telephone companies use a variety of recorded messages that inform the caller, "The number you have dialed is disconnected," or something to that effect. In other instances no connection will result or an unusual noise will be heard. When sampling in rural areas it is not unusual for nonworking numbers simply to ring without answer.

After the disposition code for ring-no-answer, the nonworking disposition code is typically the one used next most frequently. Whenever an interviewer dials a number that is not in operation, the nonworking disposition code should be recorded on the respective call-sheet. This includes those dialings in which a recorded message informs the interviewer that the dialed number has been changed (and a new number is given) or that calls are being taken by some other telephone number. For most RDD surveys, interviewers should *not* dial changed numbers because it will distort the equal probability associated with sampling. Similar to the problem associated with multiple access lines within households, if interviewers were to call changed telephone numbers, those households would have twice the likelihood of being sampled compared to households with numbers that have not been changed. Furthermore, the changed number may not ring in the sampling area.

Once a nonworking disposition results, the controller removes the call-sheet from further processing.

Temporarily Disconnected

Recorded messages that inform interviewers that a telephone number is temporarily not in service should have a separate disposition code, so that the controller can recycle the call-sheet a second time after a few days, provided the field period of the survey is long enough to justify this effort.

Nonresidential

For surveys of the general public, interviews should not be conducted at businesses or other nonresidential locations (e.g., hospitals, libraries, government offices). As mentioned earlier, AT&T statistics suggest that of all working telephone numbers in the United States, approximately one-fourth are nonresidential. Thus this disposition is a fairly common one in RDD samples.

Interviewers should be trained so they can explain *why* an interview of the general public cannot be conducted at these locations. Whenever an answering machine indicates that a business or other nonresidence has been reached, the call-sheet should be coded as nonresidential. Furthermore, if the high-pitched screech of a computer is heard, a non-residential code should also be listed on the call-sheet.

Call-sheets that result in a nonresidential disposition are then removed from further processing.

No Eligibles

Depending on the particular respondent selection requirements of a telephone survey, in some instances households will be reached that contain no eligible respondent. This outcome should be recorded on the call-sheet, and the controller should then remove it from further processing.

When conducting a general population survey with adults over 17 years of age interviewers will occasionally reach households that purportedly have no one that old living there. Given that in most such instances interviewers will be speaking with a child, these call-sheets, also coded "no eligibles," should be recycled by the controller a second time during a later interviewing session. After a second unsuccessful contact with such a household, the controller may decide to remove the call-sheet from further processing.

Contact Only

In RDD surveys that employ call-back procedures to reach respondents who are unavailable at the time of the first contact, only about half of all completed interviews occur on the first dialing. Each time an interviewer reaches a household and is told that an eligible respondent is not available at the time, the call-sheet should be coded with the contact-only disposition.

On these occasions it is critical that interviewers try to determine the best time to reach the respondent and record this information on the call-sheet; for example, "after 9:00 p.m." or "on weekends only." In this way the controller can make an informed judgment about when to recycle a particular call-sheet.

Temporarily Unavailable

Separate disposition codes should be used to differentiate those respondents who are not home at the time of an interviewer's call (as discussed above) from those who are unavailable for several days or more. This latter case may be due to brief illnesses, short vacations, week-long business trips, and so on. Providing the field period of the survey extends past the date on which respondents will be available, the controller can hold aside those call-sheets until the appropriate date for recycling.

Permanently Unavailable

In contrast to a temporary state of unavailability, there are instances when respondents are unavailable after the end of the survey's field period (e.g., an extended vacation or work-related travel out of the country). In these cases interviewers can code the disposition as permanently unavailable and the controller can remove these call-sheets from further processing, unless the field period is later extended longer than originally planned.

Handicap Barrier

Occasionally a person who meets demographic selection criteria (e.g., gender and age) is chosen as the respondent but due to some physical or mental handicap or disability cannot participate in the survey. This disposition includes a respondent who will be hospitalized beyond the field period of the survey. When such an outcome is encountered, the controller can often stop processing the call-sheet.

Sometimes, however, the incapacity is of a temporary nature (e.g., the respondent is intoxicated). In this case the interviewer must *not* conduct an interview but should note on the call-sheet that the handicap barrier is only temporary. The controller should then recycle the call-sheet at some later time in the field period.

Respondent Language Barrier

As previously described, a separate disposition code is assigned to those call-sheets in which language makes it impossible to determine if there is an eligible respondent who speaks English. In other instances an interviewer will succeed in identifying an eligible respondent within a household only to learn that *that* person cannot speak English.

For example, an English-speaking young adult (who lives with his or her parents) may answer the telephone and complete the respondent selection sequence with the interviewer. The sequence in that household may select the young adult's father, who in turn may not be able to speak English well enough to participate in the interview. This outcome should be coded as a respondent language barrier, and the controller would normally remove this call-sheet from further processing. The only exception would be a survey in which strict adherence to respondent selection criteria was unnecessary. In that case the interviewer could conduct the interview with the younger adult who spoke English.

Refusal by Selected Respondent

In surveys that use a procedure to select a specific respondent from within a household, refusal to participate will sometimes occur with the designated respondent. When this happens a respondent refusal code should be recorded on the call-sheet. This outcome differs from the case in which the refusal occurs at the household level *prior to* the selection of the actual respondent.

It is important for the controller to be able to differentiate household refusals from respondent refusals; the latter are often harder to convert since the refusal was given by the person who should be interviewed and not by a "gatekeeper" within the household. As with all refusals, interviewers should be encouraged to write a brief explanation of the nature of the refusal. This information can be quite helpful to the controller in judging how best (if at all) to recycle the call-sheet and to other interviewers in judging how to be more persuasive if subsequent attempts are made to try to convert a particular refusal.

Partial Interview

Once an interview begins it is very likely that a good interviewer can persuade the respondent to complete it. There are, however, some instances in which a respondent cannot or will not continue through to the end of the questionnaire.

In the first case, something may occur during the interview that makes it impossible for the respondent to finish *at that time*; for example, the respondent's children in another room start fighting and the respondent must go to help. If handled properly by the interviewer, these respondents are usually quite willing to be called back at another time to complete the interview. This circumstance should be coded as a partial interview, and the interviewer should note on the call-sheet when to call back. The controller should then make certain that the recontact is made at the appropriate time and, if at all possible, by the original interviewer.

The second type, in which the respondent refuses to go on and refuses to reschedule a time for a call-back, should be also be coded as a partial interview and the interviewer should note that this is actually a refusal. Experience indicates that these types of partials are often elderly respondents who get tired or become unsettled during the course of the interview. Fortunately, these types of partials do not occur often with good interviewers. When they do occur the controller may want to discuss with the original interviewer the wisdom of a call-back.

It is also possible that a partial may have resulted because of a personality clash between respondent and interviewer; for example, in the case of an elderly female who was nervous about being interviewed by a young male interviewer. Here the controller may want to reassign a call-back attempt to another interviewer.

Completion

Once an interview has been completed it should be assigned a unique disposition code to signal a stop to the processing of that particular call-sheet. It is recommended that the call-sheet then be attached to the completed questionnaire. As discussed in Chapter 6, this will facilitate verification of the completion if it proves necessary.

After the completed questionnaire has been edited for completeness and any necessary open-ended coding has been performed, a unique questionnaire identification number should be recorded on the call-sheet. In Figure 2, for example, a space is provided for this in the upper right corner.

Simplifying the Call-Sheet

For many surveys, especially those conducted by students, the use of a professional-style call-sheet, as shown in Figure 2, may be somewhat of an "overkill." If a group of interviewers is going to do only one telephone survey, and one with a relatively short field period, it unnecessarily complicates matters to expect them to use an abstract set of numerical disposition codes.

Instead, a call-sheet similar to that presented in Figure 4 should be more than adequate. With a simplified call-sheet temporary interviewers are expected to write only a brief note to the controller, explaining what happened with each dialing. Instead of listing a numerical disposition code for each outcome, they record notes such as, "no answer,", "busy," "out of service," "refused," and so on. Although this makes it somewhat more time consuming for the sampling pool's controller to sort call-sheets after each session, and the "historical information" regarding the date and time of each dialing is lost, this simplfied version works well enough for the needs of most class-related surveys.

Summary

At the end of the survey's field period, the controller ideally will have released the minimum amount of telephone numbers from the sampling pool that was needed to meet the survey's desired amount of completions. With dispositions such as nonworking, businesses, completions, and language barriers the controller stops processing those call-sheets as soon as any of these outcomes occur. New call-sheets are introduced on a limited basis in order to keep interviewer productivity at an acceptable rate, given the time within which the data must be gathered.

More troublesome are those numbers where contact has been made and yet the designated respondent has not been interviewed, and those that have continually rung but have never been answered. In most surveys it is impractical to process these call-sheets until completion has been achieved or until another final disposition (e.g., refusal) has been reached.

It is the controller's responsibility to keep the number of call-sheets that remain "in limbo" at the end of the field period to a minimum. How many of these will remain in an unresolved condition at the end of the field period will depend in part on the number of call-backs planned.

```
                    ------ User Supplied Title ------
Telephone Number
                                       Questionnaire # :  __ __ __ __
    ###-####


     * * * * * * * * * * * * * * * * * * * * * * * * * * * * * * *
     *                                                           *
     *                                                           *
     *                                                           *
     *                                                           *
     *               User's Introduction and Selection           *
     *                                                           *
     *                    Procedure Printed Here                 *
     *                                                           *
     *                                                           *
     *                                                           *
     *                                                           *
     *                                                           *
     *                                                           *
     *                                                           *
     *                                                           *
     * * * * * * * * * * * * * * * * * * * * * * * * * * * * * * *


Contact                                                    Interviewer
Attempts                        Disposition                   I.D.

    1      _____        _____

    2      _____        _____

    3      _____        _____

    4      _____        _____
```

Figure 4. Example of a Simplified Call-Sheet

From the controller's standpoint, he or she needs to make certain that each telephone number released from the sampling pool has been tried the appropriate number of times allotted for on the call-sheet.

A final comment: The use of a separate call-sheet for each telephone number should be viewed as a *necessary* but certainly not a *sufficient* condition for a final sample of good external validity. The more professional the attention given to controlling the sampling pool, the more likely this level of quality will carry over to all aspects of the telephone survey process.

EXPECTATIONS IN
PROCESSING SAMPLING POOLS

It is helpful for supervisory personnel and interviewers to have realistic expectations about the relative proportion of the various call-sheet dispositions they can expect to encounter. Otherwise they may become easily frustrated when they find that most dialings do not lead to completed interviews. For the controller it is even more important to know what to expect in order to be better able to detect problem situations before they become serious and possibly bias the final sample.

The specific distribution of dispositions of call-sheets in any given survey will depend a good deal on the efficiency of the sampling pool. RDD sampling pools that have been stratified *by prefix* according to the proportion of working telephone numbers in the sampling area associated with each prefix, and according to ranges of operating suffixes within each prefix, will contain far fewer nonworking numbers than an RDD sampling pool without any stratification. The disposition of numbers released from a sampling pool generated from a list or a directory is likely to differ from what results with RDD sampling. Also, every different geographic area that is surveyed will have its own idiosyncratic distribution of call-sheet dispositions.

The Number of Dialings Required
to Complete a Survey

Chapter 2 discussed the size of the sampling pool that should be generated for a particular survey, but this quantity is by no means the same as the number of dialings that interviewers can expect to make to reach the final sample size the surveyor desires. For example, interviewers for Groves and Kahn (1979) in their RDD sampling of the continental United States made over 44,000 dialings (i.e., dispositions) in the process of using nearly 13,000 telephone numbers (i.e., call-sheets) in order to complete 1,700 interviews.

For a more detailed look at the dialing that is required of interviewers, let us look at a three-city RDD sampling done in 1977 in Chicago, Philadelphia, and San Francisco (Skogan, 1978). The final sample included nearly 5,100 completed interviews with citywide samples in each city and 10 neighborhood samples within the three cities. Table 2

TABLE 2

Disposition of Dialings (N = 56,093) in 1977 Chicago,
Philadelphia, and San Francisco RDD Sampling

Disposition	Percentage of All Dialings
No answer or busy	38.2
Answered by nonresident or child	5.9
Non-English household or respondent	0.8
Household refusal	12.4
Nonworking	15.6
Nonresidential	4.2
Ineligible (outside sampling area)	9.3
Contact only	2.0
Respondent refusal	1.2
Partial	0.2
Miscellaneous other	1.2
Completed interview	9.1
	100.1

SOURCE: Skogan (1978).

shows the outcome of the over 56,000 dialings that were made during the field period. As noted earlier, the most frequent outcome was a ring-no-answer, which occurred in nearly four of every 10 dialings.

Several other dispositions accounted for about one in every 10 dialings. These included reaching nonworking numbers (16%), household refusals (12%; no conversions were attempted in this survey and because of rather complex geographic selection criteria used with the neighborhood samples refusals were unusually high), ineligible households (9%), and completions (9%). Table 2 also illustrates the rarity of dispositions such as language barriers, respondent refusals and partial interviews.

Still another way of looking at the nature and magnitude of the sampling process is to consider how many call-sheets reached their final disposition after one, two, three, and more dialings. Table 3 presents these results from the 1977 three-city survey. Note that two-thirds of all call-sheets reach their final disposition with *only one* dialing! In fact, those call-sheets that were recycled by the controller more than three times made up less than one-tenth of the entire sampling pool processed by interviewers.

TABLE 3
Number of Dialings Needed to Reach Final
Disposition of All Call-Sheets (N = 32,205)

Number of Calls	Telephone Numbers Requiring this Number of Calls to Reach Final Disposition		
	Number	Percentage	Cumulative Percentage
1	21555	67.4	67.4
2	4374	13.7	81.0
3	2207	6.9	87.9
4	1230	3.8	91.8
5*	1948	6.1	97.8
6	428	1.3	99.2
7	197	0.6	99.8
8	43	0.1	99.9
9	16	0.05	99.9+
10	4	0.01	99.9+
11	2	0.01	99.9+
12	1	0.00	100.0
Totals	32205	100.0	

SOURCE: Skogan (1978).
*As part of the contract with Market Opinion Research, it was agreed that any call-sheet that was dialed five times and rang without answer on each dialing would be withdrawn from further sampling. This is what accounts for the disproportionately large number of call-sheets that reached their final disposition at five dialings.

An Example of the Distribution
of Final Dispositions in an RDD Sample

Table 4 shows the *final disposition* of each call-sheet used in the 1977 three-city RDD survey—that is, the status of each call-sheet at the end of the field period. In the process of making the 56,000 dialings reported above, about 32,000 telephone numbers were used from the sampling pool. Of these 32,000 call-sheets, the most frequent final disposition was that the number was nonworking (27%). Other final dispositions that occurred with a good deal of frequency were household refusals (22%), households out of the sampling area and thus ineligible (16%), and completed interviews (16%).

Another Example

Findings from another relatively large RDD survey conducted in the metropolitan Chicago area in 1979 reinforce the pattern of dispositions

TABLE 4
Final Disposition of Call-Sheets (N = 32,205) in 1977
Chicago, Philadelphia, and San Francisco RDD Sampling

Final Disposition	Percentage of All Numbers Processed
Never answered	6.5
No adult resident ever reached	.5
Non-English household/respondent	.4
Household refusal	21.5
Nonworking	27.1
Nonresidential	7.4
Ineligible	16.2
Designated respondent never reached	.2
Designated respondent refusal	2.1
Partial	.3
Miscellaneous other	2.0
Completed interview	15.9
	100.0

SOURCE: Skogan (1978).

found in the 1977 three-city survey. Interviewing for the 1979 survey was done by the University of Illinois's Survey Research Laboratory, which processed 5,346 call-sheets for a total of 15,744 dialings in completing 1,803 interviews. In that survey there was no geographic screening of respondents into small community areas.

Similar to the ratio in the Groves and Kahn study, an average of approximately three dialings were required to dispose of the over 5,000 numbers released from the sampling pool. By far the most frequent disposition of dialings was ring-no-answer, which accounted for 38% of all dialings, the same figure found in the 1977 three-city survey. Following that, the second most frequent outcome of all dialings was to reach a household in which the selected respondent was temporarily unavailable to be interviewed; this accounted for 23% of all 15,000-plus dialings. After this, completed interviews and nonworking numbers each accounted for 11% of all dialings.

Regarding the number of dialings required for the 5,000-plus call-sheets used in sampling, nearly half (48%) were disposed of with the first dialing. In the 1979 survey, up to 10 call attempts were made before a call-sheet was removed from further processing. Because of this exhaustive attempt to interview hard-to-reach respondents, nearly 1,000 telephone numbers from the sampling pool were dialed on five or more occasions. After the tenth dialing nearly 7% of the total numbers released from the sampling pool were still unresolved; that is, the designated respondent had yet to be interviewed (n = 224) or the number had never been answered (n = 146).

Table 5 shows the *final dispositions* of all 5,346 call-sheets used in the 1979 metropolitan survey. Nonworking numbers accounted for one-third of all those released from the sampling pool, as did completed interviews. Apart from the different proportion of final dispositions that were completions or refusals, this 1979 sampling had a pattern of outcomes similar to that of the 1977 survey (compare Tables 3 and 5).

Other Experiences with the Outcomes of Sampling Pools

In the past few years the Northwestern University Survey Laboratory has conducted many RDD surveys in the Chicago metropolitan area, and the pattern of call-sheet dispositions has been found to be quite stable. Our sampling pool controller can expect about half of all call-sheets to be processed only once. Interviewers can expect better than one in three dialings, on average, to result in a ring-no-answer. We have also found that if carefully controlled, the proportion of call-sheets that reach numbers that are never answered or households in which the designated respondent is never available (even after the specified number of call-backs) can be kept to approximately 5% of the total released from the sampling pool.

In more than 30 other telephone surveys which my undergraduate and graduate classes have conducted in communities throughout the Midwest during the past six years (final sample sizes have ranged from 300 to 1,200), a fairly similar pattern of dispositions has been found. Of this group of surveys, the two extremes in experience are worth noting. On the high side, an RDD sampling of an Indiana city, in which no stratification by prefixes was done, required processing seven call-sheets for every one completion. (This is similar to the ratio in the Groves and Kahn national RDD sampling that employed no stratification by prefix.) In contrast, in an RDD sampling of one Chicago suburb in which detailed information about prefixes was used in generating the sampling pool, fewer than 2.8 call-sheets were processed for every one completion.

In sum, the scope of the work facing the controller and interviewers in RDD sampling will greatly depend on the geographic area for a particular survey and on the nature of the information known about

TABLE 5
Final Disposition of Call-Sheets (N = 5,346)
in 1979 Chicago Metropolitan Area RDD Sampling

Final Disposition	Number	Percentage of All Sample Numbers
Numbers not in service	1765	33.0
No answer after 10 calls	146	2.7
Business and group quarters numbers screened out	571	10.7
Needed foreign language interviewers	132	2.5
No one 19 years or older	19	.3
No household respondent reached	33	.6
Refusal by household respondents	337	6.3
Selected respondents never reached	224	4.2
Refusal by selected respondents	216	4.0
Breakoffs during interview	98	1.8
Completed interviews	1803	33.7
Other final dispositions	2	.0

SOURCE: Lavrakas et al. (1980).

prefixes that was used to generate the sampling pool. If full information about each prefix in the sampling area is employed in generating the sampling pool, one can anticipate over a 50% reduction in the number of call-sheets that will be processed compared to unstratified RDD sampling.

Compared to RDD sampling, if a sampling pool is generated from a list or directory, relatively fewer call-sheets will be processed to achieve a desired number of completions. Yet even with up-to-date lists it is not unusual that between 50% and 100% more call-sheets will be needed for processing than the total number of completions planned. As with RDD sampling, the length of the field period will affect how many call-sheets remain unresolved when interviewing stops.

A note on panel studies. In concluding this section a comment can be made about what to expect with telephone panel studies, those that reinterview respondents after some scheduled time lag. Our experience shows that interviewers' success in reinterviewing an original respondent will depend largely on residential mobility patterns within the sampling area (Lavrakas & Maier, 1984). In the central city about 60% of the original respondents can be found and reinterviewed after a one-year time lag; in suburban areas this figure is closer to 70%. (In general upwards of 90% of those respondents who can be reached at wave 2 of a panel study can be successfully reinterviewed. The remainder refuse or are never available during the survey's field period.)

SAMPLING POOL DISPOSITIONS
AND SURVEY RESPONSE RATES

A major reason to employ a highly controlled system for processing sampling pools is to achieve as high a response rate as possible within a given sampling area. This section, however, is not meant to be an exhaustive discussion of telephone survey response rates. Through the use of an example I will illustrate some of the issues that should be considered. Currently most survey professionals agree that response rates are best thought of as a range rather than as a single value. For those seeking additional discussion of these issues, see Frey (1983) and Fowler (1984).

For illustrative purposes results from the 1979 Chicago metropolitan RDD survey discussed in the previous section will be used. Referring back to Table 5, one can see the distribution of all 5,346 call-sheets (i.e., telephone numbers) used in that survey. This sampling pool was generated using information about nonoperating banks of suffixes within the over 400 prefixes that served the sampling area but not with information about the relative number of residential access lines on each prefix. That is, the sampling pool was *not stratified* by prefix, but dialing was made more efficient by concentrating it within each prefix's working banks of suffixes.

Sampling Pool Efficiency Rates

Table 6 shows various response rates associated with this survey. Different response rates can be calculated depending on what is used as the numerator and denominator. For example, a partial measure for the efficiency of the sampling pool in reaching working numbers is 67% (i.e., 3581/5346 = .6698). Thus only 1,765 numbers, or 33%, released from the sampling pool were confirmed as nonworking. In this respect the sampling pool was very efficient, despite the fact it was not stratified by prefix.

As a measure of the efficiency of the sampling pool in reaching residential households, a conservative estimate would be to subtract

TABLE 6
Completion Rate Calculations

Type of Rate	Comparison	Numerator/ Denominator	Rate (%)
Gross efficiency of sampling pool	Working numbers/ All numbers	3581/5346	67.0
Efficiency of sampling pool in reaching households	Possible households/ All numbers	3010/5346	56.3
Conservative estimate of efficiency of sampling pool in reaching households	Probable households/ All numbers	2864/5346	53.6
Gross completion rate	All completions/ All numbers	1803/5346	33.7
Conservative completion rate	All completions/ All possible households	1803/3010	59.9
Most reasonable completion rate	All completions/ All eligibles	1803/2713	66.5
"Best" potential completion rate	All potential completions/ All eligibles	1951/2713	71.9

SOURCE: Lavrakas et al. (1980).

only the 571 call-sheets that reached nonresidential numbers from the numerator, and not the 146 call-sheets that were never answered after 10 dialings. This would leave 3010/5346, or 56%. Yet in all likelihood most of these never-answered telephones were not residential numbers.

The field period for this survey extended for seven weeks, during which time each of these numbers was tried 10 times, on various days of the week and weekend, and at various times of the day and evening. Thus it is reasonable to assume that the bulk of these numbers rang at coin telephones, in warehouses, or other nonresidential locations, or were not in operation. Following this reasoning, these 146 call-sheets should be subtracted from the numerator, which leaves a more conservative rate of 54% for the efficiency of the sampling pool in reaching residential numbers within this sampling area.

Completion Rates

To calculate a gross completion rate, one could compare the 1,803 completions to the entire set of 5,346 call-sheets used. As shown in Table 6, this yields a rate of about 34%. A more reasonable but still quite conservative estimate of the success of this survey in completing interviews at residential numbers would be to use all possible household numbers (including never-answered) in the denominator. This yields a ratio of 1803/3010, or 60%. Finally, the most reasonable completion rate is probably one that eliminated from the denominator those numbers that can be argued to be ineligible. This would include households in which no one met the age requirements, the designated respondent could not speak English, and numbers that were never answered after 10 different call attempts. Using this mode of calculation, two of every three eligible respondents (66%) were successfully interviewed.

Another response rate can be calculated which takes into account the reality of a *finite* field period and makes an assumption about the eventual success that may have been achieved in interviewing those respondents who were never reached during the field period. If two-thirds of those 224 designated respondents who had yet to be interviewed when the survey's field period ended had eventually given an interview, then the numerator could be inflated by 148 to yield a potential 1,951 completions. The best potential response rate would then be estimated at about 72%. If closing the gap between the most reasonable response rate (66%) and this best potential response rate were important to the surveyor, a decision could be made to extend the field period to try to succeed with these hard-to-reach respondents.

Rates of Noncompletions

Other rates that are often calculated have to do with the relative nature of noncompletions. Table 7 shows a detailed breakdown of all noncompletions for the 1979 survey. About one-third of these occurred because some gatekeeper in the household refused to go through the respondent selection procedure with the interviewer. In cases in which a designated respondent was identified within a household, proportionally fewer refused; this accounted for about 20% of noncompletions. A similar proportion of noncompletions occurred because the field period came to an end without ever reaching the designated respondent, even after 10 dialings.

A refusal rate for this survey could be estimated by comparing the 1,803 completions with the 651 call-sheets that ended in some form of refusal (see Table 5 for household refusals, respondent refusals, and partials). Using 2,454 (1803 + 651) as the denominator and 651 as the numerator, the refusal rate was about 27%.

TABLE 7
Reasons for Noncompletions (N = 1052)*

Source of Noncompletions	Percentage of Noncompletions
Non-English-speaking households	12.5
Selected respondent never located	22.2
Selected respondent refused	20.5
Breakoff of interview	9.3
Household respondent never located	3.1
Household respondent refused	32.0
Other disposition	.2

SOURCE: Lavrakas et al. (1980).
*These are the dispositions of the last calls made to households for which no completed interview was secured.

Summary

At the end of the field period there are a variety of ways to measure the efficiency of the sampling that was completed. It is good practice to calculate these rates to provide information regarding the relative success of the survey in reaching a truly representative sample within the sampling area. Those publishing the results of their surveys are also encouraged to report many of these rates so that others can assess the relative quality of the sampling that occurred.

EXERCISES

1. Using the dispositions shown in Figure 3 as an example, develop a category system that would have interviewers use 10 or fewer disposition codes. Explain your reasoning for collapsing categories.

2. Compose the text of a standardized spiel for interviewers to leave on residential answering machines. Keep it to about 50 words or fewer.

3. Write two scenarios that demonstrate your understanding of the difference between a household refusal and a respondent refusal.

4. Calculate each of the response rates shown in Table 6 using the data given in Table 2.

5. Prepare a table of noncompletions as shown in Table 7 using the data given in Table 2.

4

SELECTING RESPONDENTS

Properly selecting an eligible respondent within the sampling unit (typically a household) is another important aspect of quality telephone surveys. Contrary to popular opinion, most telephone surveys should not be structured in a manner that allows interviewers to interview the first person who answers the telephone or to choose whomever they want to interview within the sampling unit. This chapter discusses many approaches to systematic selection of eligible respondents within sampling units and discusses the importance of the survey's introductory spiel in establishing rapport between the interviewer and respondent.

Those unfamiliar with valid telephone methods often erroneously assume that the first person who answers the telephone is the one who is interviewed. This is not the case in any survey designed to gather a representative sample of the population of interest. Instead, some form of systematic respondent selection procedure must be employed.

This chapter covers various issues concerning the representative selection of a respondent *within* a sampling unit, such as a household. The manner in which the survey is introduced when contact is first made with a household is often critical to overall compliance and particularly to the successful resolution of respondent selection. Therefore, introductory spiels for telephone surveys are also addressed.

The chapter begins with a review of the importance of controlled (systematic) selection of respondents for telephone surveys. The following section addresses the importance of the introduction that interviewers use to establish rapport quickly at the point of contact. Included in this discussion is an explanation of the need to train interviewers to be prepared to respond with standard answers to common questions asked by respondents about the survey. Following this, the remainder of the chapter reviews some frequently employed respondent selection techniques.

STARTING OFF
ON A SOLID FOOTING

As stated in Chapter 3, refusals to telephone surveys are most likely to occur at the very beginning of interviewer contact rather than after a designated respondent has come to the telephone or after the questionnaire has been started. Thus the first 30-60 seconds of contact are very important.

How, then, does a surveyor balance two important agendas that occur simultaneously at the beginning of the interview? That is, the surveyor typically wants to end the field period with as demographically representative a final sample as possible, but techniques that are likely to choose *the most representative* demographic mixture from the population are typically those that take longest to employ and are most likely to cause suspicion because of their intrusive nature.

The skill of interviewers does much to determine the success of any survey in balancing these tensions. But even excellent interviewers will have trouble if an introductory spiel is awkward or if the respondent selection method is worded in a confusing or threatening fashion. In contrast, even inexperienced interviewers can be quite successful if they are trained to use properly a well-worded introduction and persuasive selection procedure.

Obviously, when sampling is done from a list and the respondent is a particular individual whose name is known, "respondent selection" merely requires that interviewers ask for that person by name. But in many instances with list sampling and with all RDD sampling, interviewers will not know the name of the person *within* a sampling unit (e.g., household) who should be interviewed. Therefore, any survey designed to gather precise univariate estimates of person-level population parameters must employ a systematic selection technique to maximize external validity (i.e., generalizability).

As mentioned earlier, surveys that interview the first person who answers the telephone and who sounds old enough to answer the questions are not likely to gather data that validly reflect the attitudes, behaviors, experiences, and so on of the population of interest. Surveys that allow interviewers to speak with whomever they want within a sampling unit will also suffer from this problem. For example, imagine a survey in which interviewers spoke with the person at each sampling unit most willing to be interviewed at the time. This approach may please interviewers, but is likely to have disastrous consequences on the representativeness of the final sample. Therefore, respondents should be selected in a systematic and unbiased fashion, which means interviewers cannot choose *for themselves* the person within a sampling unit whom they want to interview.

Respondents can be selected within a sampling unit in a truly random fashion, but surveyors will not always need or want to employ such a rigorous approach. Rather, for the purposes of most surveys it will be acceptable to use a technique that balances selection along the lines of both *gender* and *age*. Because most sampling units (such as households) are quite homogeneous on most other demographic characteristics, representative sampling *of units* should provide adequate variation from within the population on other demographic factors. For example, an accurate racial mixture within a sampling area should result directly from the approach used to generate the sampling pool, not because race was a characteristic upon which respondents were selected from within households.

On the other hand, race may be a characteristic along which a survey needs to *screen* respondents and thus by default needs to screen households, given that there are so few racially heterogeneous ones. In this case, interviewers will need to determine a potential respondent's race *before* the first item of the questionnaire is asked to determine if the respondent is eligible. Thus a selection technique may also have to be worded so that it picks only certain *types* of respondents.

INTRODUCING THE SURVEY

There are differing opinions among survey professionals regarding how much information should be given in the spiel that is used to introduce the survey. I side with those who believe it should be as brief as possible so that the respondent can be actively engaged via the start of the questionnaire. Exceptions to this rule always exist, as in the case in which the introduction must contain instructions regarding how the questionnaire is organized or about unusual types of questions.

I also agree with Frey (1983) that an introductory spiel should contain enough information to reduce as much as possible any nervousness on the part of the person answering the telephone who hears that a stranger is calling to conduct a telephone survey. In other words, the credibility of the interviewer (and thus the survey) must be established as soon as possible, and it is the task of the introduction to do this.

At the same time, experience demonstrates that getting someone's full cooperation is easier once he or she begins the questionnaire. The longer the introduction, the more a potential respondent must listen without active involvement, the greater the chance he or she will get "turned off" before questioning even begins (Dillman, Gallegos, & Frey, 1976). Thus whenever possible, and especially if a surveyor has any doubts, an introductory spiel should be pilot-tested along with the rest of the selection technique and the questionnaire itself.

Developing An Introductory Spiel

Surveyors may differ in the exact way they prefer to word introductions, but the following information should always be considered for inclusion:

(1) verification of the telephone number dialed by the interviewer;
(2) identification of the interviewer and the interviewer's affiliation;
(3) brief explanation of the purpose of the survey and its sampling area; and
(4) some "positively" worded phrase to encourage cooperation.

Figure 5 shows an example of an introduction/selection sheet with a typical introductory spiel used at our survey lab. A copy of this sheet is attached to every call-sheet released from the sampling pool. The introductory statement in Figure 5 begins with a verification of the telephone number. Then the interviewer introduces herself or himself *by name*, identifies where the call is originating, and explains why the call is being made. Included in the wording about the purpose of the call is a reference to the sampling area. Whenever possible some implicit or explicit statement should be made about the use of the survey, unless it might confound the answers given by respondents.

If the questionnaire is a short one (10 minutes), there is no reason not to mention its brevity in the introduction. On the other hand, if the interview will take in excess of 15 minutes, I suggest that no statement be made about the time required unless a respondent asks pointedly how long it will take. In that case all interviewers should be trained to give the same (honest) answer through use of a standardized "fallback" statement; these statements are discussed below.

Fallback Statements

In most cases it is simply unnecessary, and thus inadvisable, to devise an introductory spiel that contains a detailed explanation of what the survey is about. If the respondent wants to know more about the survey before making a decision about whether or not to participate, interviewers should be given an honest, standardized explanation to read.

Introduction/Selection Sheet: Evanston 1981 Survey

Hello, is this _____? [VERIFY TELEPHONE NUMBER]

My name is _____, and I'm calling from the Northwestern University
Survey Laboratory. We are conducting a short random survey of Evanston
residents in cooperation with the Evanston Police Department. The purpose of
the survey is to determine how people feel about the safety and security of
their neighborhoods, so that the City can plan better anti-crime programs.
Your cooperation is voluntary, but we'd greatly appreciate your help.

```
* * * * * * * * * * * * * * * * * * * * * * * * * * * * * * *
*                                                           *
*                                                           *
*                                                           *
*                                                           *
*                                                           *
*                                                           *
*                                                           *
*              User Supplied Selection Procedure            *
*                                                           *
*                                                           *
*                                                           *
*                                                           *
*                                                           *
*                                                           *
*                                                           *
*                                                           *
*                                                           *
*                                                           *
*                                                           *
* * * * * * * * * * * * * * * * * * * * * * * * * * * * * * *
```

Figure 5. Example of an Introductory Spiel

For those respondents who seem reluctant to participate, interviewers
should, at their own discretion, read the detailed explanation of the
survey's purpose.

As mentioned before, it is at the beginning of the contact period—
that is, during the introduction—that most persons make their decision
about whether or not to cooperate with the interviewer. Although it is
recommended that the standard introduction be brief, interviewers
must also be trained to provide honest, standardized answers when
respondents (or gatekeepers) want more information before agreeing to
cooperate.

Three basic types of questions are sometimes asked of interviewers. The word "sometimes" is important to keep in mind: If interviewers were nearly always asked these types of questions, then it would be wise to incorporate answers into the introductory spiel. However, as in the majority of cases interviewers will not need to give out a more lengthy explanation, it expedites matters by not reading detailed information to everyone because not everyone will need or want to hear it, and the interviewer may risk losing the respondent before even getting started with the questionnaire. The three types of information that are sometimes asked include

(1) What is the purpose of the survey and how will the findings be used?
(2) How did you get my telephone number?
(3) Who is conducting this survey?

For each of these questions fallback statements should be provided to interviewers, to enable them to give honest, standardized answers to respondents who ask them. Figure 6 provides an example of a typical fallback sheet. In all cases the explanations should include a reminder that the answers to the questionnaire are confidential and the respondent's cooperation is voluntary.

RESPONDENT SELECTION TECHNIQUES

Even in the most poorly controlled telephone surveys there often is a selection of respondents from among the members of a sampling unit. (Remember that this section assumes that interviewers are not contacting persons whose names have been sampled from a list.) Even an untrained interviewer will normally recognize that a potential respondent must be physically and intellectually able to answer the questionnaire. In some cases, however, common sense does not seem to prevail, and interviews will be attempted with persons who can barely understand English or those whose temporary or permanent mental capacity is diminished beyond the point of providing valid answers.

It is not the purpose of this section to discuss ways to guard against these errors in judgment on the part of interviewers; this will be addressed in Chapters 5 and 6. Rather, this section will review different respondent selection procedures and discuss what can be expected with the use of each.

C25 INTERVIEWER FALL-BACK SHEET

Explanation of Survey: The survey is very short, about two or three minutes. Most of the questions deal with your opinions about heart transplant operations. It's important that we speak with people regardless of how much they think they know about these operations, so that we can get a true picture of attitudes throughout Chicago. I'm taking a course at Northwestern called 'Advanced Reporting', and my class is conducting this survey as part of our course work. All your answers are confidential, your cooperation is voluntary, but I'd greatly appreciate your help.

Use of Survey: As part of my course, I have to write a news story for my professor about the results of this survey. As a class, we have to interview several hundred Chicago residents. All answers will be grouped together; no responses will be identified with any specific person. Your cooperation is voluntary, but I'd greatly appreciate your help.

Random-Digit Dialing: Your number was chosen by a technique called 'random digit dialing'. My professor put all the 3-digit telephone exchanges that ring in Chicago into a computer, and the computer randomly added 4 more digits to make up 7-digit phone numbers . . . That's how we reached your home . . . We use this technique because it's important that we speak with people throughout the City of Chicago, regardless whether their number is listed or unlisted. That's the only way we can get a survey that will fairly represent the opinions of Chicago residents.

Female/Male Selection: I have a sheet here that tells me the one person in your home whom I can interview. Sometimes it picks the oldest or youngest woman to be interviewed, while other times it picks the oldest or youngest man. This is the only way we will get a fair balance of younger and older females and males.

Check-up: If you have any questions about this survey, you can contact my professor, Dr. Lavrakas ("love-rack-us"), at 491-5662 during the daytime.

Figure 6. Example of Fallback Statements

Although never a recommended approach, it is instructive to begin by looking at the uncontrolled procedure that simply leaves it up to interviewers to decide whom to interview within a sampling unit, if for no other reason than to inform the reader of the problems it can create. The discussion to follow assumes that the telephone survey being conducted will be an interview of individuals reporting on their *own* attitudes, behaviors, experiences, and so on. If the purpose of a survey is to measure some construct that exists at the level of the sampling unit (e.g., number of bathrooms with tubs or showers in a dwelling unit), then any knowledgeable household informant can be interviewed without biasing the survey's findings. In this case respondent selection from within a sampling unit is simply a matter of the interviewer asking for any eligible person as defined by the surveyor. An easy and controlled approach in this case is to have interviewers ask for the "woman of the household" if the telephone is answered by a woman, or the "man of the household" if it is answered by a man.

Uncontrolled Selection

In general population surveys in which there is no structured selection, interviewers simply try to interview anyone in the household who qualifies as an eligible. For example, age is the typical factor by which interviewers make their selections: any person over the age of 12 or 17, or some other age delimiter. In contrast, a survey may be a sampling of males' opinions, and interviewers need speak with any male who is available in the household, if there is one. (Telephone surveys for market research dealing with traditional "masculine" products, such as chewing tobacco, often employ this uncontrolled selection of adult males.) Other surveys may simply have interviewers speak with a head of household (or the head of household), often allowing the household to define what this means. In each instance in which a formal selection process is not printed on the introduction/selection sheet, interviewers merely ask to speak with any person fitting the eligibility requirement(s) immediately after they have read the introductory statement.

Two types of problems can be created with uncontrolled respondent selection when a survey's purpose is to measure the level at which some variable exists within the population of the sampling area. First, and the more serious, is that a representative sample from the population of interest is not likely to be drawn. If interviewers are allowed to choose whomever they wish who fits the eligibility requirements, the resulting sample will be disproportionately made up of those persons who are more likely to be available at the time interviewers call. In the general population, this often means women and older adults (see Salmon & Nichols, 1983). If several people are available and fit the eligibility requirements, then interviewers will naturally want to speak with the most cooperative one—in other words, the one most willing to be interviewed. If this happens, then the resulting sample will be more likely to include younger and better-educated persons. Unfortunately, the selection biases associated with availability and willingness cannot be expected to cancel each other out. Rather, the mix that will result will not be predictable from survey to survey and cannot be defended as scientific or having high external validity.

The second problem with uncontrolled selection is one that may grow in time. As the public becomes more knowledgable about valid survey methods, it is hoped that a survey of the general population that employs uncontrolled respondent selection will be regarded as "unprofessional" by more and more persons. As it is in the best interest of both interviewers and the survey to impress upon potential respondents that they will not be wasting their time by participating in a sloppy (i.e., likely to be invalid) survey, compliance should be higher with a well-worded, nonintrusive, yet nonetheless *formalized* selection procedure.

Controlled Selection

This section begins by discussing three systematic approaches to stratifying respondent selection within a sampling unit, such as a household, based on gender (female/male) and age (oldest/youngest). With each of these methods, if only one person is available (e.g., as in single-person households), that person automatically becomes the designated respondent.

Each of the methods has the limitation of never sampling middle-aged persons within households with three or more persons (adults) of the same gender. For example, with each of these methods an adult woman who lives in a household with both an older and younger woman (i.e., three adult females) will be missed by each selection method. The same holds true for males in households of parallel gender compositions. However, households with three or more adults of the same gender are quite rare in the general population, and the convenience provided by these selection methods is generally accepted as a benefit that outweighs the cost of missing such potential respondents.

Troldahl-Carter-Bryant (T-C-B) method. Prior to the mid-1960s, the standard approach to selecting a respondent from within a household in face-to-face interviewing was to begin the interviewing process with an enumeration of all eligibles ordered by gender and age. Kish (1949) developed this random selection method, discussed later in this chapter. Recognizing that refusals typically occur at the beginning of interviewer contact, Troldahl and Carter (1964) proposed a less intrusive method for systematically (not randomly) selecting a respondent. Bryant (1975) suggested a modification of the Troldahl-Carter method to compensate for an undersampling of males. As described here, the T-C-B selection method reflects a further refinement based on the findings of Czaja, Blair, and Sebestik (1982).

The T-C-B method requires the interviewer to ask two selection questions: (1) "How many persons ___ years or older live in your household, including yourself?" and (2) "How many of these are women?" The age delimiter used in the first question is determined by the needs of each particular survey, but in most cases it is 18 (i.e., adults are selected).

One of four versions of a selection matrix is then used by interviewers to select objectively the designated respondent. These versions are shown in Figure 7. Versions A and B will oversample males, whereas versions C and D will oversample females. Used in proper combination throughout the field period, the four versions will ideally yield a mix of males and females that approximates their true proportion within the population that is being sampled. (The reader is reminded that of all adults in the United States, about 54% are women, and this preponderance of adult females is even greater in some urban areas.)

Theoretically, the proper combination for using the different versions is to print one per introduction/selection sheet, as shown in Figure 8, and pair these with call-sheets that are used in sampling, according to the following order: A, B, C, D, A, B, C, A, B, C, D, A, B, C, and so on. That is, version D is only used one-seventh of the time to compensate for what otherwise would result in an oversampling of women. In practice, however, even this combination of versions often undersamples males, so it is recommended that the controller take a daily count of males and females, compare it to the known ratio within the sampling area, and correct for discrepancies by selectively introducing either more or fewer new call-sheets with version D attached to bring the male/female mix back in line. For example, if after three days of a field period that will last two weeks 60% or more of the completions are with females, in a sampling area where only 55% of the adults are women, then the controller could withhold the release of new (i.e., unused) call-sheets with version D of the T-C-B selection matrix until a more proper gender ratio is achieved.

It is worth noting that in their controlled comparison of the T-B-C selection method and the Kish method, Czaja et al. (1982) found that only when T-B-C used the word "women" in the second question did it produce fewer refusals than the Kish approach. When T-B-C's second question was worded to ask, "How many of these are men?" the refusal rate was not different than with the Kish approach.

A final consideration in the use of a respondent selection method such as the T-C-B approach regards the need for interviewers to be trained to use a fallback statement explaining its purpose. Although use of a fallback statement will not be necessary in most cases, there are times when either the gatekeeper or the designated respondent will ask why only a certain person can be interviewed. Sometimes an interviewer

Number of Women 18+ in Household		Number of Persons 18+ in Household			
		1	2	3	4 Or More
Matrix A	0	man	oldest man	oldest man	youngest man
	1	woman	man	youngest man	woman
	2		youngest woman	man	youngest man
	3			oldest woman	man or youngest man
	4+				youngest woman
Matrix B	0	man	youngest man	youngest man	oldest man
	1	woman	woman	oldest man	woman
	2		oldest woman	man	oldest man
	3			youngest woman	man or oldest man
	4+				oldest woman
Matrix C	0	man	youngest man	oldest man	oldest man
	1	woman	man	woman	youngest man
	2		youngest woman	oldest woman	oldest woman
	3			oldest woman	youngest woman
	4+				youngest woman
Matrix D	0	man	oldest man	youngest man	youngest man
	1	woman	woman	woman	oldest man
	2		oldest woman	youngest woman	youngest woman
	3			youngest woman	oldest woman
	4+				oldest woman

Figure 7. T-C-B Selection Charts

SOURCE: Czaja et al. (1982).

Hello, is this _____ ? [VERIFY TELEPHONE NUMBER]

My name is _____ , and I'm calling from . . .   * * * insert user's introductory spiel * * *

How many adults 18 years of age or older are presently living in your household, including yourself? _____ [CIRCLE IN COLUMN A]

How many of these adults are women? _____ [CIRCLE IN ROW B]   MATRIX B

Row B	Col. A	Number of Adults In Household		
Number of Women in Household	1	2	3	4 or more
0	man	youngest man	youngest man	oldest man
1	woman	woman	oldest man	woman
2		oldest woman	man	oldest man
3			youngest woman	man or oldest man
4 or more				oldest woman

NOTE: The intersection of Col. A and Row B determines the sex and relative age of the respondent to be interviewed

[IF DESIGNATED RESPONDENT OTHER THAN PERSON TO WHOM YOU ARE SPEAKING ASK FOR THAT PERSON AND REPEAT INTRODUCTION BEFORE BEGINNING QUESTIONNAIRE]

[IF DESIGNATED RESPONDENT NOT HOME, DETERMINE WHEN BEST TO CALL-BACK AND RECORD INFORMATION ON CALL-SHEET]

Figure 8. Introduction/Selection Sheet with T-C-B

must defuse hostility before the gatekeeper will agree to summon the designated respondent. Such hostility appears to stem from a perception that the answerer's opinion doesn't count and that is why the interviewer is choosing someone else in the household. This problem seems to occur most often with either women who resent the idea that the interviewer may ask for a man or with males who do not like their wives to express their own opinions. Thus a standardized response, such as the following, can be quite helpful for interviewers:

> I have a sheet here that tells me the *one* person in your household whom I can interview. Sometimes this sheet picks a woman, and other times it picks a man. *Only* by using this method to select people to interview in each household we contact will we end our survey with a *fair and proper* balance of females and males.

Modified T-C-B method. In some instances the T-C-B is overly complicated for use with inexperienced persons who may be interviewing for only one or a few sessions; for example, as part of a short class project. In order to give inexperienced interviewers an easier selection method while at the same time not wanting to lose control of respondent selection entirely, I recommend employing two versions of an all-purpose, combined call-sheet and introduction/selection sheet, as shown in Figure 9.

In using this method interviewers merely ask to speak with a male or a female in households with one such person (as with T-C-B) or ask to speak with the *youngest* male or female in households with more than one person of the same gender. There are two versions of this selection method: one that selects a female when there is at least one in the household and one that selects a male. When this selection technique is used in surveys that last only a few days and thus can employ only a few call-backs, the effect of this oversampling of younger adult men and women often results in a preferred age mix, given that these persons (especially younger adult males) are those hardest to reach, and will otherwise be undersampled when the field period of a survey does not allow for numerous call-backs. As with the full T-C-B method, a daily tally of males and females is recommended with this modified approach to determine the need to adjust the proportion of call-sheets that select for males.

Hagen and Collier method. In the same way that Troldahl and Carter proposed a less intrusive respondent selection method than the Kish method, which was assumed to produce lower refusal rates, Hagen and Collier (1982) have proposed a selection method that is even less intrusive than the T-C-B approach. Rather than following the intro-ductory statement with a request for the number of persons over some

------ User Supplied Title ------

PHONE NUMBER

###-####

Hello, is this _____? [VERIFY TELEPHONE NUMBER]

My name is _____, and I am a journalism student at
Northwestern University. My class is conducting a very short public opinion
survey about heart transplant operations.

For this survey, I need to speak with the YOUNGEST WOMAN in your household, if
there is one.

[IF SPEAKING TO YOUNGEST WOMAN, SKIP TO Q1]

[IF SHE IS UNAVAILABLE, DETERMINE WHEN BEST TO CALL BACK]

[IF NO WOMAN IN HOUSEHOLD, ASK TO SPEAK TO YOUNGEST MAN -- IF HE IS NOT
 AVAILABLE, ASK WHEN BEST TO CALL BACK]

[WHEN SELECTED RESPONDENT COMES TO PHONE, REPEAT INTRO IF NECESSARY, THEN
 SKIP TO Q1]

	DISPOSITION	ID#
ATTEMPT #1:	_____	___
ATTEMPT #2:	_____	___
ATTEMPT #3:	_____	___
ATTEMPT #4:	_____	___

Figure 9. Example of a Modified T-C-B with Call-Sheet

age criterion, the Hagen-Collier approach simply asks outright for one of four types of respondents, thereby avoiding the need to determine the number of possible eligibles in the household at the beginning of interviewer contact.

Four versions of an introduction/selection sheet are used. Each is printed so that interviewers ask to speak with either the youngest female/woman, oldest female/woman, youngest male/man, or oldest male/man. Depending on the age limit for eligibles, a particular survey may want to employ the terms "female" and "male" whereas another may want to use "woman" and "man."

As shown in Figure 10, if the sampling unit does not contain a person of the gender asked for, then interviewers need to be given proper follow-up instructions on the introduction/selection sheet. With the Hagen-Collier method it is important that interviewers understand that

---

1984 Election Survey Selection Page: Version Y-M

Hello, is this _____? [VERIFY TELEPHONE NUMBER]

My name is _____, and I'm calling from the Northwestern University
Survey Lab in Evanston, Illinois. We are conducting a survey of Cook County
residents to find out their opinions about the November presidential election.

For this survey, I need to speak with the youngest adult male in your
household over the age of 17, if there is one.

[IF YOUNGEST MALE IS AVAILABLE, REPEAT INTRO IF NECESSARY AND GO TO Q1]

[IF YOUNGEST MALE IS UNAVAILABLE, DETERMINE WHEN TO CALL BACK AND LIST ON
CALLSHEET]

[IF NO MALE IN HOUSEHOLD]:

Then may I please speak with the youngest adult female?

[IF YOUNGEST FEMALE IS AVAILABLE, REPEAT INTRO IF NECESSARY AND GO TO Q1]

[IF YOUNGEST FEMALE IS UNAVAILABLE, DETERMINE WHEN TO CALL BACK AND LIST ON
CALLSHEET]

Figure 10. Example of Hagen and Collier Introduction/Selection Sheet

in a household with only one woman, she is both the youngest *and* the
oldest woman. If this is not understood by interviewers, they in turn will
not be able to explain it to respondents, who sometimes seem to
interpret "youngest" to mean "young" and "oldest" to mean "old." For
example, if the selection sheet instructs interviewers to ask for the
youngest woman and they are told by an elderly female, "there's no
young woman living here," interviewers must be able to correct this
misunderstanding so that a proper respondent selection can be made.

Hagen and Collier (1982) did not present explicit examples of how to
word their selection technique; however, Figure 10 shows one way to
employ this method. The wording attempts to clarify the age range that
is being considered, and also attempts to clarify the issue that it is the
youngest or oldest man/woman who is home *at the time* but rather the
one who lives in the household.

As with the T-C-B method, the four versions of the Hagen-Collier method must be used in a ratio that yields a close approximation of the known distribution of males and females in the sampling area. On most occasions if the four versions are used in equal proportion, there will be an undersampling of males, which will require increased usage of those introduction/selection sheets that ask for males. Similar to T-C-B, the Hagen-Collier method also misses middle-aged persons in households with three or more eligibles of the same gender.

Kish method of random selection. The most rigorous respondent selection method that is the accepted standard for face-to-face interviews was developed by Kish (1949, 1965). It can also be used in telephone surveys that require as complete a representation as possible of all eligibles from within sampling units; that is, surveys in which it is important to include those middle-aged persons in households in which three or more eligibles of the same gender live. (Actually the Kish technique leads to an extremely small underrepresentation of the youngest of eligibles in households with more than six eligibles.)

As shown in Figure 11, immediately after the introductory spiel the interviewer must determine all the eligibles at the sampling unit. In most cases this means determining all those who meet some age criterion living in a household. Some surveyors prefer to have interviewers identify eligibles by the relationships within the household; other surveyors have interviewers ask for eligibles' first names. Either way, it is typical for interviewers to begin by identifying the household head(s) and then follow by listing other eligibles. For example, assuming the survey is sampling adults, an interviewer will most commonly begin by recording the "husband" and the "wife," as this is the most frequent adult composition in U.S. households.

After the interviewer has made certain that all eligibles are listed, the age of each of the eligibles is requested and recorded. The interviewer then pauses to check that the age of each person listed meets the age requirements of the survey, eliminating those that do not from further consideration. During the pause the interviewer assigns a rank-order number to each eligible according to the following rule: oldest male numbered 1, next oldest male (if there is one) numbered 2, and so on through all males listed, then followed by oldest female, the next oldest female, and so forth.

For example, consider a household composed of a husband, wife, their adult son, their adult daughter, and the husband's father (as shown in Figure 11). In this case the father of the husband is assigned 1, the husband 2, the son 3, the wife 4, and the daughter 5.

Fortunately for those surveys that use the Kish method, more than 90% of all households have three or *fewer* eligibles so that the time it takes interviewers to list eligibles and their ages and to assign a selection number is relatively short. In face-to-face interviews the household informant can see what the interviewer is doing. When the Kish method is used on the telephone, it is prudent to have interviewers make a brief comment, as illustrated in Figure 11, to alert the listener as to why there is a slight pause at this point.

After the numerical selection number is recorded for each eligible, the interviewer consults one of eight versions of a selection table that is printed on the introduction/selection sheet (see Figure 11). This selection table indicates which of the eligibles is the designated respondent. In the selection table in Figure 11, an interviewer who had reached a household with five eligibles would interview the wife (4).

Figure 12 shows the selection information that should be printed in each of the eight versions of the selection table used with the Kish method. The first column in Figure 12 also indicates the proportion which each table is used within the survey. In manually pairing introduction/selection sheets with call-sheets the following order of selection tables would be used: A, A, B_1, B_2, C, C, D, D, E_1, E_2, F, F.

As can be seen, the Kish technique requires interviewers to request rather personal information of the household informant very early after contact has been made. Good interviewers will be successful with Kish despite its difficulty. Less skilled interviewers, especially those without experience, are likely to have a high refusal rate and furthermore will often not use the method properly. It is the responsibility of the surveyor to determine whether the needs of the survey justify the costs that might be associated with use of the Kish selection method via telephone.

Birthday methods for random respondent selection. Recently, different approaches for yielding a random selection of respondents within sampling units have been explored (Oldendick, Sorenson, Tuchfarber, & Bishop, 1985; O'Rourke & Blair, 1983; Salmon & Nichols, 1983). These methods either ask for the person within the sampling unit whose birthday was most recent or ask for the person who will have the next birthday.

Theoretically these methods represent true random selection, but in practice there is still some uncertainty whether this in fact results.

Hello, is this _____? [VERIFY TELEPHONE NUMBER]

My name is _____, and I'm calling from . . .   * * * insert introductory spiel * * *

In order to randomly pick one person in your household whom I can interview I need to begin by
listing all the persons in your household 18 years old or older. Could you just tell me their
relationships to each other, not their names. [AFTER LISTING PERSONS IN COLUMN 1 BELOW CONTINUE,
UNLESS ONLY ONE ADULT, THEN DETERMINE AGE AND GO TO Q1:] Now I need to know the age of each person.
[AFTER LISTING AGES IN COLUMN 2 BELOW CONTINUE:] Now it will take me just a few seconds to use a
selection chart I have here to determine the person I'm supposed to interview in your household.

LIST ALL PERSONS AGE 18 AND OVER IN DWELLING UNIT   NUMBER PERSONS 18 OR OVER IN THE
                                                         FOLLOWING ORDER --

Relationship to Head (1)	Sex (2)	Age (3)	Adult (4)	Check (5)
HUSBAND	M	52	2	
WIFE	F	50	4	✓
SON	M	23	3	
DAUGHTER	F	19	5	
HUSB. FATHER	M	78	2	

OLDEST MALE, NEXT OLDEST MALE, ETC.;
FOLLOWED BY OLDEST FEMALE, NEXT OLDEST
FEMALE, ETC. THEN USE SELECTION TABLE
BELOW TO CHOOSE RESPONDENT.

SELECTION TABLE D

IF THE NUMBER OF ADULTS IN THE DWELLING IS:	INTERVIEW THE ADULT NUMBERED:
1	1
2	2
3	2
4	3
5	4
6 or more	4

The selection chart indicates that in your household I'm supposed to interview _____? May I
please speak with (her)(him)?

[IF DESIGNATED RESPONDENT IS SOMEONE OTHER THAN WHOM YOU ARE SPEAKING WITH, ASK TO SPEAK WITH THAT
  PERSON AND REPEAT INTRO BEFORE SKIPPING TO Q1]

[IF DESIGNATED RESPONDENT IS UNAVAILABLE, DETERMINE WHEN BEST TO CALL BACK AND LIST ON CALL SHEET]

Figure 11. Example of Kish Selection Sheet

Because these birthday selection methods are nonintrusive, not time
consuming and easy for interviewers to use, their appeal is great.
Telephone surveyors should follow the methodological research literature over the next several years to determine the validity of the birthday
techniques.

Proportions of Assigned Tables	Table Number	If the Number of Adults in Household Is:					
		1	2	3	4	5	6 or More
		Select Adult Numbered:					
1/6	A	1	1	1	1	1	1
1/12	B1	1	1	1	1	2	2
1/12	B2	1	1	1	2	2	2
1/6	C	1	1	2	2	3	3
1/6	D	1	2	2	3	4	4
1/12	E1	1	2	3	3	3	5
1/12	E2	1	2	3	4	5	5
1/6	F	1	2	3	4	5	6

Figure 12.   Kish Selection Tables

SOURCE: Kish (1965).

Other Criteria for Respondent Selection

When a survey requires a certain type of respondent—that is, not merely a systematically selected person from within the household—then other selection methods will need to be employed. For example, some surveys will need to interview only heads of households, or taxpayers. Others will need to interview only persons who live within some relatively small geographic boundary. Still others will want to select some unique subsample of the general population.

Selecting for head(s) of household. The definition of who qualifies as a head of the household has been changing since the early 1970s. Traditionally the head of the household was defined as the husband when such a person existed, as was the case in about three of every four households as recently as the 1950s. Nowadays a more accepted and egalitarian definition defines "heads of household" as both the female and male in a "primary couple" in households with married or cohabiting adults. As has always been the case, in single adult households that adult is the head. Often if a survey needs to select taxpayers (e.g., a mayor wants the opinions of this constituency before issuing a policy statement), then selecting for head of household will yield a representative sample.

If a surveyor wants a fair balance of male and female heads of households, a selection method such as that shown in Figure 13 can be used. Somewhat similar to the Kish method, the interviewer begins by asking for an enumeration of all adults based on their relationship to one another. In most cases it will then be obvious who is (are) the head(s). If there is any uncertainty, the interviewer must determine which person or couple is economically dominant, thus defining the head.

Two versions of this selection method are printed and paired with call-sheets. One version, as shown in Figure 13, asks for the male head in households with a primary couple; the other version asks for the female head. When we employ this selection technique we print these versions on pink and blue stock to further reinforce for interviewers which head will be the designated respondent in a household with a primary couple. In households with only one head, that person is designated as the respondent regardless of the color stock on which the form is printed. printed.

When a survey selects for head of household, it is not unusual to sample females 60% of the time or more, especially in urban areas where mothers are the heads of many single-parent households. Demographic patterns within the sampling area should be known so that the controller can adjust the use of the different versions if daily tallies of males and females indicate an unrepresentative gender ratio.

Geographic screening. Sometimes a telephone survey will reach households that are outside the boundaries of the sampling area because prefix boundaries do not always coincide with those of the sampling area. In the case in which the boundaries of the sampling area coincide with municipal boundaries, geographic screening is fairly easy to employ. Immediately after the introductory spiel, the interviewer merely asks, "Do you live in _____?", where the blank contains the name of some recognized area (e.g., Cook County, Wayne County, Boston, San Jose, etc.). If the person being spoken to indicates that the household is not located in the specified area, the interviewer politely explains why the interview cannot be conducted before hanging up. If the household informant is uncertain whether the household is located within the sampling area, the interviewer should ask to speak with some other knowledgeable person in the household.

In all cases in which a household is excluded because the interviewer is told it is located outside the specified area, a special disposition code is needed for the call-sheet. The controller can then sort call-sheets for this disposition, noting if there are more of these ineligibles than had been expected. If there is uncertainty about the accuracy of the household informants in responding to the geographic screener, then some proportion of these dispositions should be checked via a reverse directory.

```
                 ------ User Supplied Title ------


Hello, is this _____?  [VERIFY TELEPHONE NUMBER]

My name is _____, and I'm calling from . . .


In order to systematically select which adult to interview in your household,
would you please tell me how many adults 18 years old or older live there?

              _____# OF ADULTS 18 YEARS OR OLDER


[IF "ONE", ASK FOR THAT ADULT, REPEAT INTRO IF NECESSARY, AND SKIP TO Q1]


I don't need any names but would you also tell me their relationship to each
other?

[ENUMERATE ADULT MEMBERS OF HOUSEHOLD (E.G., "HUSBAND", "WIFE", "HUSBAND'S
FATHER", ETC.]:


        ___(1)_____
        ___(2)_____
        ___(3)_____      ** INTERVIEW HUSBAND/MALE
                                               IN PRIMARY COUPLE **
        ___(4)_____
        ___(5)_____
        ___(6)_____


[IF PRIMARY COUPLE NOT CLEAR, PICK ECONOMIC DOMINANT BY ASKING]:

Who provides the major share of financial support for the family?


[CHECK RESPONDENT, THEN CONTINUE]:

For this survey I need to interview _____. May I please speak with
(him)(her)?

[IF DESIGNATED RESPONDENT IS UNAVAILABLE, DETERMINE WHEN BEST TO CALL BACK AND
LIST ON CALL-SHEET]
```

Figure 13. Example of Head of Household Selection

It is possible that some potential respondents will be mistaken in answering that they do not live within the sampling boundaries. Therefore, if it is found that a sizable proportion (say, over 20%) of the ineligibles are actually eligibles, then a decision can be made on how to deal with this problem. If a pilot test is done, then the geographic screener can also be tested. If the problem is detected after the field period is under way, then the controller may be faced with the onerous task of trying to verify the eligibility status of each of these dispositions.

Even more troublesome are sampling boundaries that conform to neither prefix boundaries nor municipal boundaries. For example, in the 1977 survey of Chicago, San Francisco, and Philadelphia discussed in Chapter 3, 10 inner-city neighborhoods were oversampled. For each neighborhood a series of geographic-locator questions were asked immediately after the introductory spiel. An example of this (for the South Philadelphia neighborhood) is shown in Figure 14. If a household was not within the sampling boundaries, contact was politely terminated.

Unfortunately, not all persons seem to be well acquainted with the location of their own household in relation to directional references, such as north or east of some designated street. Furthermore, this type of complicated and intrusive questioning, coming at the beginning of contact before trust in the interviewer has developed on the part of the household respondent, often leads to disproportionately high refusal rates (as was experienced in the 1977 three-city survey). Thus the validity of small-area geographic screeners is often questionable, especially with RDD, and should always be validated in a pilot test before being used in the actual survey.

Selecting for other factors. Within reason, respondents can be sampled along several factors not simply demographic ones. Through careful development and pilot testing a surveyor should be able to devise a workable selection sequence without jeopardizing response rates.

In those instances in which selection criteria are complicated, it may be wise to intersperse them in the early sequencing of questions, with an understanding that the interview will be terminated if it is determined that the respondent is not really an eligible. In other words, it may be necessary to bear the cost of starting the interview with persons who may not be eligible, rather than loading all selection criteria at the point of contact, thereby producing too many refusals by asking too many personal questions before establishing interviewer-respondent rapport.

For example, Figure 15 shows a selection sequence that was used to screen for any male in a household over 24 years of age whose racial/ethnic background was black or white and who was not of Arab or Jewish descent. The sequence of questions has the interviewer first ask to speak with a male, 25 years of age or older, if there is one. In

Hello, is this _____? [VERIFY TELEPHONE NUMBER]

My name is _____, and I'm calling from . . .

G1. In this survey we need to get the opinion of people who live in the South Philadelphia Area. Do
     you live between Morris (on the north) and Packer Avenue (on the south)?

                                      YES 1
                                      NO. . . . . 2 [POLITELY TERMINATE]
                                      DON'T KNOW. . . . . . . 7 [SKIP TO G3]

G2. Do you live between 5th (on the east) and Vare Avenue (on the west)?

                                      YES . . . . 1 [SKIP TO SELECTION]
                                      NO. . . . . 2 [POLITELY TERMINATE]
                                      DON'T KNOW. 7

[NOTE: PACKER AVENUE IS NORTH OF FDR PARK: VARE AVENUE IS JUST EAST OF THE SCHUYLKILL RIVER]

G3. Well, can you tell me which street you live on? [IF NOT INCLUDED IN LIST BELOW, POLITELY
     TERMINATE AS WRONG NEIGHBORHOOD]

G4. Would that address be between _____? [READ RANGE FROM LIST; IF NOT IN RANGE, POLITELY
     TERMINATE AS WRONG NEIGHBORHOOD]

STREET . . . . .NUMBER		STREET . . . . .NUMBER		STREET . . . . .NUMBER	
(North-South)		(North-South)		(East-West)	
Alder	1700-3000 S	Opal	1700-3000 S	Barbara	500-3000
Bailey	"	Percy	"	Bigler	"
Bambrey	"	Reese	"	Cantrell	"
Bancroft	"	Ringgold	"	Castle	"
Beechwood	"	Rosewood	"	Daly	"
Beulah	"	Sartain	"	Dudley	"
Bonsall	"	Sheridan	"	Durfor	"
Bouvier	"	Stoker	"	Emily	"
Broad	"	Taney	"	Fitzgerald	"
Bucknell	"	Taylor	"	Gladstone	"
etc.	"	etc.	"	etc.	"

* * * CONTINUE WITH SELECTION PROCEDURE * * *

Figure 14. Example of Geographic Screening

households without such a person, contact is politely terminated. Once
the interviewer reaches a male of appropriate age, the additional
demographic screening questions for race, ethnicity, and religion are
asked. If at any point in this sequence it is determined that the person is
ineligible, contact is terminated.

This selection sequence works quite well even though it requires
interviewers to speak with more males than will be eligible. Never-

Hello, is this _____? [VERIFY TELEPHONE NUMBER]

My name is _____, and I'm calling from the Northwestern University
Survey Lab. We are conducting a public opinion survey about international
affairs and the Middle East.

For this survey, I need to speak with a man, 25 years of age or older. Does
anyone in your household fit into this category?

[IF TOLD NO MAN LIVES IN HOUSEHOLD, POLITELY TERMINATE]

[IF MAN IN HOUSEHOLD IS NOT 25 YEARS OR OLDER, POLITELY TERMINATE]

[IF ELIGIBLE MALE IS NOT HOME, DETERMINE WHEN TO CALL BACK]

****

[CONTINUE WHEN SPEAKING TO ELIGIBLE MALE, REPEAT INTRO IF NECESSARY:]

In addition to questions about international affairs and the Middle East,
throughout the survey I will also be asking you some questions about yourself.
Now I'll begin by asking you three short background questions.

S1. What is your racial background? Are you . . .

                              Asian, ... 1 [POLITELY TERMINATE]
                              Black, ... 2 [SKIP TO S3]
                              Hispanic, or . . . . . 3 [POLITELY TERMINATE]
                              White? 4
                              OTHER. . . . . 5 [POLITELY TERMINATE]
                              REFUSED. . . . . 8 [POLITELY TERMINATE]

S2. Are you of Arabic or Jewish decent?

                              YES. . . . . 1 [POLITELY TERMINATE]
                              NO 2
                              REFUSED. . . . . 8 [POLITELY TERMINATE]

S3. What is your religious preference? Are you . .

        Catholic,. 1
        Protestant,. 2
        Jewish, or . . . . 3 [POLITELY TERMINATE]
        Something else? (specify _____).4
        REFUSED. . . . . 8 [POLITELY TERMINATE]

Figure 15. Example of Screener Selection Sheet

theless, this approach is far better than one that would follow the
introduction by stating, "For this survey, I need to speak with any male
in your household, over the age of 24, who is black or white, but not an
Arab or a Jew, if there is such a person." Not only would a sequence like
this frequently be misunderstood, but interviewers would still have to go
through the three screener questions to make absolutely certain they
were speaking with an eligible.

Other, even more involved selection criteria can be used effectively in telephone surveys. Through the use of a pilot test the surveyor should be able to refine the wording so as not to increase the refusal rate. Ultimately it is the ability of interviewers to use the required selection procedure that will play a large part in determining how many potential respondents are lost due to refusals shortly after contact.

EXERCISES

1. Write an introductory spiel for an RDD survey designed to sample adults' satisfaction with local government services within a local municipality (county, city, or town). The survey is being commissioned by the local municipality's governing body (e.g., county board, mayor's office, or town council).

2. Using the introductory spiel written in exercise 1, develop an introduction/selection sheet that utilizes any of the controlled selection methods reviewed in this chapter to select one adult per household sampled.

3. Continuing from the two previous exercises, write the text of a fallback statement for use by interviewers if they were asked by potential respondents how their confidentiality will be protected if they participate in this survey commissioned by the local government. Direct the fallback statement especially to those who are apprehensive that their names may be given to the local governing body. Limit the fallback statement to 100 words or less.

4. Contact a local marketing research firm and determine the respondent selection method(s) they typically employ with general population surveys, and why they prefer this(these) method(s). Explain your findings in a written narrative, including any critique you feel necessary of the firm's choice(s).

5. For a national RDD survey measuring shopping habits, write and lay out an introduction and a respondent selection sequence that will screen for the following type of eligible: a woman, 21-59 years of age, who also is at least a high school graduate.

6. Modify the selection sequence developed in exercise 5 so that it also screens out all persons who do not have an American Express card, a MasterCharge card, *or* a Visa card.

5

SUPERVISION I: STRUCTURING INTERVIEWERS' WORK

The quality of data that will be gathered via a telephone survey is directly related to the quality of interviewing that is performed. This in turn is a function of the skill of individual interviewers and the rigor of the systematic routine that interviewers are expected to follow. This chapter reviews considerations in the hiring and training of telephone survey interviewers. Where appropriate, distinctions are made between the use of paid and unpaid interviewers.

Interviewing is part of the telephone surveying process that is much more a craft than a science. This chapter discusses the importance of the interviewer in telephone surveys. Here the purpose is to inform the reader about the ways in which a surveyor can structure various stages of the survey process, ranging from interviewer recruitment to on-the-job-training, to obtain interviewers who will produce data of the highest possible quality.

The chapter begins with a brief discussion of the issue of control of interviewing quality in telephone surveys as opposed to personal interviewing. Next, considerations are reviewed about the ways in which paid and unpaid (volunteer) telephone interviewers can be recruited. Included here is advice on how to screen potential interviewers before making a final decision to use them for a survey.

The importance of an interviewer training session prior to the start of each survey is reviewed. A detailed explanation is then provided about the two basic parts to each training session: the general and the survey-specific. The chapter concludes with a discussion of the never-ending aspect of on-the-job training.

QUALITY CONTROL IN TELEPHONE VERSUS PERSONAL INTERVIEWING

This text has emphasized that the great advantage telephone surveys have over other forms of gathering survey data is the opportunity for control provided by a centralized data collection process. If this control is properly exercised, the resulting data can be of the highest possible quality apart from any limits in the way the sample was generated or in the manner the questionnaire was formulated.

Surprisingly, although many surveyors appear to recognize the importance of a good sampling pool and a good questionnaire, they are often lax in the control they exercise over the telephone interviewing process. It is as though they assume that once one has a good questionnaire and a valid sampling procedure, successful data collection is guaranteed. The reality of gathering survey data via telephone, however, shows the folly of this assumption: Unless data are gathered in a controlled and standardized fashion, they will not be comparable across respondents, thereby invalidating the survey.

One of the reasons for the apparent lack of adequate attention given to rigorous control in telephone surveys may be that many surveyors have learned about survey methods through books about and experience with face-to-face interviewing. With personal interviewing the role of interviewers and supervisors in collecting data differs in significant ways from telephone interviewing. For example, with face-to-face interviewing it is impossible to check completed questionnaires immediately and provide immediate feedback to interviewers. Personal interviewing also does not allow for the supervisor to monitor the progress of ongoing interviews.

Because of these and other factors the interviewer plays a much more active role in "creating" the data in personal interviewing than needs to be accepted in telephone interviewing. No matter how superior a group of interviewers, the level of standardization that will be achieved with face-to-face interviews will not approach what can and should be expected with centralized telephone interviewing.

RECRUITMENT AND HIRING
OF INTERVIEWERS

General Considerations

A first consideration regarding interviewers is whether they are paid for their work or are unpaid, such as volunteers or students who must do interviewing as part of coursework. When a survey employs paid interviewers, there should be a greater likelihood of higher-quality interviewing due to several factors.

First, in situations in which interviewers are paid, there can be careful selection of the most skilled individuals. In situations with unpaid interviewers there is much less control over who will *not* be allowed to interview. Second, paid interviewers are more likely to have an objective detachment from the survey's purpose. In contrast, unpaid interviewers often have expectancies about the data; that is, volunteers by nature are often committed to an organization's purpose in conducting a survey and may hold some preconceived notion of the results. Similarly, students who interview for academic credit often have an interest in the survey's outcome, especially when it is their own class's survey.

Regardless of whether interviewers are paid or unpaid, it is recommended that each interviewer enter into some type of written agreement with the surveyor. This agreement should include a clause about not violating confidentiality. Although this suggestion may be standard practice for those who employ paid interviewers, it is rarely the approach taken by those who utilize unpaid interviewers. Yet the National Organization for Voluntary Action (NOVA) strongly recommends that volunteers be treated like paid employees when it comes to holding them accountable for what they have volunteered to do. NOVA believes that having volunteers sign a *nonbinding* work contract can be a very effective technique in reinforing the importance of the work the volunteer has agreed to do. That is, unpaid interviewers need to know their time is not being wasted, and a written contract is a symbolic affirmation of the importance of the work.

Interviewers' training should be consistent regardless of whether they are paid or unpaid, but *recruitment* takes a somewhat different tack depending on which type of interviewer is being sought, though there are some constants that should be included in the recruitment of all interviewers. First, it must be made very clear to all interviewers that telephone surveys normally require a highly structured and "sterile" style of interviewing; one that does not allow for creativity on the part of interviewers in the ordering or wording of particular questionnaire items or in deciding who can be interviewed. Furthermore, all prospective interviewers should be informed about the constant monitoring done by supervisors, including listening to ongoing interviews.

Informing prospective interviewers of these features *in advance* of making a final decision about their beginning work will create realistic expectancies. In the case of the paid interviewer, it may discourage those who do not conform to highly structured situations from applying. Additional considerations for each type of interviewer follow.

Paid Interviewers

With paid interviewers the surveyor has the chance of getting the most qualified individuals. Thus the recruitment and hiring process should be structured with this goal in mind. This can best be achieved by using a careful screening process and by offering a good wage to attract persons with greater ability and experience who might otherwise not be interested in telephone interviewing. Simply stated, the more one pays interviewers, the more that can be reasonably expected from them, both in terms of quality and quantity. It is even possible that total interviewing costs will be lower when a survey employs relatively fewer "expensive" yet skilled interviewers whose productivity and quality are high than when more "inexpensive," less skilled interviewers are used.

In the hiring of new interviewers advertisements should mention the starting wage and the part-time nature of the work. It is also recommended that the phrase, "experience preferred" be included because it helps to screen out some marginal applicants. In the hiring ads used by the Northwestern University Survey Lab, we list an hourly wage range that is approximately twice the current minimum wage. Our willingness to pay interviewers this well reflects the quality of interviewer we want to employ.

The ad should also list a telephone number to call to apply, not an address to visit in person. There is an explicit purpose in screening potential telephone interviewers via telephone. In this way the applicant can be assessed on "telephone presence." An interviewer screening form can be printed that includes first-impression ratings about the applicant's verbal demeanor along with whatever other demographic and back-ground information is needed from applicants. The more experienced the managerial personnel who screen applicants, the more valid the ratings. If prospective interviewers were to apply *in person,* nonverbal behavior would be confounded with any assessment made. Because it is the applicant's voice, not her or his appearance, that will affect success as a telephone interviewer, there is little reason to see the applicant.

Overall the manner in which hiring and training are organized should result in a "self-selection" process that leads applicants who are not likely to be good interviewers to decide for themselves to withdraw their application. Based upon the preliminary screening interview, applicants who are judged to have potential are chosen for training. The self-selection process continues to work at this point. If during the application interview it is made clear that *reliability of attendance* is a very important employment criterion (i.e., showing up for every interviewing session that one is scheduled for), prompt attendance to the training session(s) is another way to judge the attractiveness of a particular applicant. After this, on-the-job performance should be used to decide who to continue to employ as an interviewer.

Unpaid Interviewers

There is less control over persons who are available to serve as interviewers when a survey cannot or does not pay for their time. In the situation in which students must do interviewing as part of a class project, all students must normally participate. In this case the surveyor has to make do with whoever is enrolled. With volunteer interviewers, self-selection and screening criteria such as those discussed above for paid interviewers can be employed. In other words, a surveyor must always be ready to tell a volunteer that he or she may be better suited for some other type of service and should not try to interview.

THE TRAINING SESSION

A training session should be held before each new survey commences. The purpose of training sessions is to provide interviewers (and supervisors) with enough background information that they are well prepared to begin on-the-job training or actual interviewing. The information that should be given to interviewers is of two types: (1) general information about standard work expectancies and (2) specific information about the particular survey.

Training sessions should always be conducted by skilled personnel, preferably the survey's field director. This person should be experienced with all aspects of the survey process, ideally having been both a telephone interviewer and a supervisor. The trainer must be articulate and organized: able to communicate with interviewers in a structured fashion while at the same time flexible enough to deal with un-anticipated issues that may arise during the training session. Ultimately it is the trainer's responsibility to instill the importance of quality interviewing in those being trained.

Training for General Work Expectancies

The following issues should be addressed in that part of training that covers general work expectancies:

(1) what makes a good telephone interviewer;
(2) how interviewing is monitored, including an explication of standards for quality and quantity; and
(3) the particulars of employment with the organization or person conducting the survey.

Quality telephone interviewing. Every training session should include a discussion or review of what behavioral characteristics are possessed by a good interviewer. The reader may diasagree with some of the specific suggestions made below, but it can be agreed that interviewers need to know what verbal behavior is expected of them.

A good telephone interviewer properly uses the call-sheet, introduction and selection procedure, fallback statements, and questionnaire in an energetic fashion that does not sacrifice quality for quantity. Therefore, interviewers must be trained to realize that there is a lot more to quality telephone interviewing than merely asking questions and recording answers. The particulars concerning a survey's specific disposition codes, introduction, selection procedure, fallback statements, and questionnaire should be saved for the second part of the training session. In the first part of training interviewers should learn about the "generic" aspects of all the steps that make up the total interviewing process.

A good measure of interviewer productivity is to compare the number of *properly completed* interviews attained per interviewing session with the number of refusals and partials the interviewer experiences. (A good standard for which interviewers should strive is to achieve four completions for every one refusal or partial.) Interviewers should be told this, with emphasis on what "properly completed" means, and should be provided an explanation of why refusals are harmful to the survey's purpose.

Instruction should also be provided about speaking in a pleasant manner, without also biasing (i.e., reinforcing) certain types of responses. For example, interviewers should be warned against becoming an "on-the-phone therapist" when respondents want to go beyond the specifics of the questionnaire to discuss their own opinions or problems in detail. In general, this means that interviewers must constantly strive to retain control of the pacing and flow of the survey process. (Ideally the questionnaire will be constructed in a way that helps the interviewer retain this control.)

In most survey situations interviewers should basically serve as *intelligent automatons*. They should not let their own personalities bias answers by being either too enthusiastic or too detached. A balance must be struck between these two extremes so that respondents can give their own answers uninfluenced by any expectancies they may perceive on the part of interviewers.

At the same time respondents must know they are being interviewed by another person, not by some impersonal recording machine. An interviewer must be allowed and should be expected to show some personal judgment as to how to handle different types of respondents but without making comments that are likely to bias responses. In this first part of training, the trainer should also explain how interviewers are expected to "probe" respondents who have answered in some irrelevant or ambiguous fashion; again, without biasing responses.

Handling refusals. The single factor that seems to differentiate the best of interviewers from those who are not good is the ability to handle difficult respondents and outright refusals. The part of the training session that covers general expectancies should therefore include a detailed discussion of the nature of refusals and advice on how to be "politely persuasive" without being overly aggressive. Most experienced surveyors have their own preferred approach on how they want their interviewers to handle difficult respondents. My advice is to assume that every potential respondent needs to be given some incentive for participating.

With most respondents sufficient incentive is generated by telling them they are being helpful by providing answers. For others it appears to make them feel important to know that it is *their* opinions that are being sought. But for about two or three of every 10 potential respondents, interviewers will have to work harder at selling the interview. In these difficult cases one option is to assume that the timing of the contact is wrong and to call back on another occasion. Interviewers may be trained to make a statement such as, "I'm sorry we've bothered you at what apparently is a bad time for you." Interviewers can then continue by either asking if there is a better time to call back or by simply stating that a call-back will be made, or by not saying anything else. Here it remains the responsibility of the trained interviewer to determine what is likely to be the best way to respond in each individual case.

Another option is to "plead" with the potential respondent. When a telephone questionnaire is a relatively short one (i.e., 10 minutes or less), an interviewer can try to convince a reluctant respondent that it will not take very long. Another tactic that might be used to counter reluctance is to state that any question that the respondent is uncomfortable answering may be left unanswered. Or interviewers can be trained to give several levels of assurance of both the legitimacy and importance of the survey. Here it is useful for interviewers to be able to provide the survey sponsor's name and telephone number in case the respondent wants further verification. Often, however, simply providing such assurances goes a long way toward relieving the concerns of reluctant respondents.

A last resort to consider is for interviewers to remind the respondent that by cooperating the respondent is helping the interviewer earn a living. (Or for the unpaid interviewer, cooperation is helping the interviewer fulfill her or his obligation.) By personalizing the issue of cooperation, the interviewer is neither referring to an abstract incentive, such as "to help plan better social programs," nor appealing in the name of a third party (the survey's sponsor). Rather, the reluctant respondent may be persuaded to feel the satisfaction of knowing that he or she is directly helping the person who is doing the interviewing. (As is discussed later in this chapter, the mode of payment used with interviewers will often affect the resourcefulness with which interviewers pursue refusals.)

Role playing. Role-playing opportunities should also be built into the part of the training session that deals with general work expectations. For example, interviewers can practice trying to gain cooperation from a reluctant respondent whose role can be played by the person conducting the training session.

Regardless of what the trainer decides to do in this part of the training session, interviewers should recognize (and ideally internalize) that they are responsible for leaving all persons they contact with a good impression of surveys. In other words, interviewers "owe" it to the survey profession to avoid leaving respondents with a bad taste for telephone surveys.

Explaining the system of supervision. The part of training that addresses general work expectancies should also explain the supervisory system that will be employed to monitor interviewing quality. For purposes of illustration, differences in the role of the supervisor in face-to-face interviewing and in telephone interviewing can be compared. Emphasis here should be on the high degree of supervision that centralized telephone interviewing affords and how it relates to data quality.

Interviewers should be reminded of the structured routine they will be expected to follow—for example, call-sheets will be assigned to them, specific disposition codes will be used, numbers must be verified after the telephone is answered, a selection procedure will single out one eligible person per household, and so on—and that it is the responsibility of the supervisor to see that this routine is followed properly. Interviewers should also be told of the many ways in which supervisors check the quality of their interviewing. First, completed questionnaires should be turned in to supervisors for immediate review to *validate* their completeness. Second, a centralized telephone bank ideally will allow supervisors to listen in, at random, to all aspects of the interviewing process. Interviewers should be told that this occurs primarily so that supervisors can provide them with constructive feedback. Finally, interviewers should be made aware that a small proportion of their completions will be chosen for *verification* by supervisory personnel—someone will call the respondent back to verify that the interview was properly completed.

In explaining to interviewers why this intensive level of monitoring is desirable, the trainer should link it to the need professionally to guarantee the survey's sponsor that high-quality interviewing occurs. It should not be made to appear to interviewers that they are not trusted, but rather that supervisors will be assisting them to do the best possible interviewing.

Interviewer productivity. Along with letting interviewers know how their work is monitored, they should be told what is expected of them in terms of quality and quantity. From the standpoint of quality, emphasis should be placed on closely following the routine for processing call-sheets, selecting respondents, answering respondents' questions, and administering the questionnaire. Interviewers should also be told that daily tallies of their productivity are taken and that their refusal rate will be compared to their completion rate. A field director should have a good notion of the average number of completions that an interviewer should attain per session (which will differ by survey depending on the efficiency of the sampling pool, the complexity of the respondent selection criteria, and the length of the questionnaire), so this figure should be communicated to interviewers, with emphasis on quality rather than quantity.

Interviewers should recognize that if they consistently receive too many refusals, their continued tenure is unlikely. As previously mentioned, I recommend that interviewers be told to strive to maintain at least a 4:1 ratio between completions and refusals. When sampling is done primarily in urban areas this ratio may be unrealistically high, yet it is still a desirable goal for interviewers to set for themselves.

Finally, the speed at which call-sheets are processed should be mentioned. They are not expected to rush from one dialing to another, but interviewers should be told that there should be no appreciable delays between dialings.

Payment and other employment practices. The final points that should be discussed by the trainer regarding general work expectancies deal with the specific employment practices used by whoever is conducting the survey: what employment forms should be filled out, how work schedules will be assigned, what the attendance policy is, and how and when interviewers will be paid or credited for their work in the case of unpaid interviewers.

The issue of payment is a critical one that deserves its own review. Psychologically, the manner in which interviewers are paid ideally should reflect the expectancies that are held of them. The standard approach to paying interviewers is with an hourly wage. The reasoning behind the practice of paying interviewers by the hour, regardless of their productivity, is that it often has been assumed to be the best way to emphasize quality over quantity. If interviewers were paid exclusively on a *per completed interview* basis, the thinking goes, they would be reinforced to work as fast as possible, thus sacrificing quality.

This *is* the reasoning held by many survey professionals, but it denies the ability of a highly structured supervisory system to ensure quality interviewing under different modes of payment. Given that many survey professionals developed their expertise in conjunction with in-person interviewing, in which the constant supervision of ongoing interviews is not possible, it too often has been assumed that the way one pays interviewers for face-to-face interviewing is also the best way to pay telephone interviewers. My experience in the past nine years with telephone surveys has led me to choose a different method of payment, which is linked to the intensive level of supervision that should always be instituted in telephone surveys.

I recommend a mixed mode of payment, in which the majority of income earned by interviewers comes from a standard hourly wage but in which a proportion of their wages is also based on their productivity. In general a 2:1 balance seems to be a good one: For example, interviewers might be paid $4 per hour and earn an additional $2, on average, based on their own productivity. Psychologically, this mixed mode reflects the fact that most surveys are not conducted by well-funded survey organizations that can afford the luxury of employing interviewers who may be slow but still do acceptable quality interviewing. All interviewing must be of acceptable quality; however, the mixed mode payment recognizes that the best interviewers also seem consistently to average more completions with fewer refusals. By providing a monetary increment for each completion, a more equitable reward structure is instituted.

I have used this mixed mode of payment of interviewers for the past five years (prior to that I employed the traditional hourly wage approach). In that time I have never received a complaint from the over 100 interviewers I have employed that this mode of payment is unfair. Although this approach to payment requires more record-keeping than with a standard hourly wage, it reflects the individual attention that I believe is consistent with expectations of interviewing quality. It is this personalized approach to remuneration that realistically allows a survey organization to expect the best from its interviewers.

In sum, interviewers should be explicitly trained to recognize that they can earn a good income provided they conform to the standards of those responsible for conducting a survey. High-quality telephone interviewing is not easy work; as such, good interviewers appear to appreciate the opportunity to have their earnings partly reflect their job performance.

Training for the Specifics
of a Particular Survey

Interviewers who are familiar with a survey organization's or surveyor's general work expectancies need not attend the first part of training. But all interviewers must be trained to understand the particulars of each new survey. Generally, this second part of the training session should be structured as follows:

(1) an explanation of the purpose of the survey;
(2) a review of how telephone numbers will be processed;
(3) an explanation of the use of the introduction/selection sheet;
(4) a review of all fallback statements; and
(5) a detailed explanation of the questionnaire, including practice in its use.

A standard approach that should always be followed is to have an interviewer training packet for each person who will be working on a survey. This packet contains examples of the forms that will be used in the survey and instructions to supplement what will be explained orally in the training session.

Purpose of survey. By understanding the purpose of the survey, interviewers are more likely to believe in the importance of the data they are gathering. This belief can provide interviewers with a sense of confidence that comes from knowing they are engaged in meaningful work that someone (the survey's sponsor) sincerely cares about. As such, it is recommended that the sponsor attend the training session and explain the survey's purpose. Not only is the sponsor most knowledgable about the survey's purpose, but, as important, it provides interviewers an opportunity to meet the person for whom they are indirectly or directly working.

The explanation of purpose given to interviewers need not be too detailed. Furthermore, it should not be decided arbitrarily whether specific research hypotheses (if there are any) should be shared with interviewers. If there is a chance that this type of knowledge may bias data by creating expectations on the part of interviewers, it is probably wise not to provide it. On the other hand, it can undermine interviewers' ability to persuade reluctant respondents if they are kept completely ignorant of the survey's purpose.

The particular call-sheet. Next, the call-sheet that will be used in the survey should be discussed, particularly noting the number of call-backs that will be used for hard-to-reach respondents and any other differences from other call-sheets interviewers may have used. Interviewers should be reminded that they are expected to fill out the date, time, and their ID number *before* each dialing. Specific disposition codes should be reviewed but discussed in detail only if they are ones with which interviewers are not already familiar.

Introduction/selection sheet. After reviewing the specific call-sheet, an explanation of the introduction/selection sheet should be presented. Depending on the complexity of the selection procedure, the trainer may choose to engage some interviewers in a form of role-playing, taking on the part of a potential respondent and having several different interviewers (one at a time) use the selection procedure. This often helps to highlight any difficult parts of the selection procedure and reinforces for interviewers that they need practice in its use before their first interviewing session.

Fallback statements. Because questions from gatekeepers and potential respondents are most likely to arise while the interviewer is using the introduction/selection sheet, it is at this point in the training session that specific fallback statements should be discussed. The nuances of each of these standardized responses should be pointed out. Again, interviewers should be reminded to practice using these statements *before* coming in to interview.

The questionnaire. At this point of the training session the trainer should proceed through the questionnaire, item by item, reading most items in their entirety (including the response options) to provide an example to all interviewers on the use of the questionnaire. Skip patterns that require interviewers to ask different questions depending on certain responses need special attention. If open-ended questions are included in the questionnaire, the trainer must explain the type and amount of detail that is expected that interviewers will *legibly* write down. (The amount of space that is physically provided on the questionnaire to record open-ended answers structures an expectancy on the part of interviewers regarding how much should be written.)

After a detailed review of the questionnaire, role-playing should again be used. Interviewers should be separated into groupings of five or fewer and assigned to practice the questionnaire with a supervisor taking on the role of a respondent. Practice with the questionnaire should proceed in a round-robin fashion, following skip patterns depending on the responses given by the supervisor. (Interviewers enjoy this part of training sessions because it allows for their active involvement.) In general, role-playing should last approximately 30-60 minutes depending on the length and complexity of the questionnaire. It is not the purpose of role-playing to make interviewers expert with the questionnaire but to help bring out any uncertainties they may have about its use.

Ending the training session. The training session is concluded with a review of what was covered and a reminder of the importance of the interviewer becoming very familiar with all the materials in the training packet *before* coming in to interview. The trainer should also allude to the nature of the on-the-job training that will be done.

ON-THE-JOB TRAINING

Although the training session plays an important role in informing interviewers about all aspects of the survey process, the best training occurs during actual interviewing. Those familiar with telephone surveys know that interviewers typically take one or two interviewing sessions to "hit their stride" with each new survey. Recognizing this, an ideal (albeit costly) approach to training is to have at least one practice session of actual interviewing for each interviewer before the interviewer starts to generate completions that count toward the survey's final sample size. In a sense this is similar to a pilot test but not one that is used to refine the questionnaire further. Instead these on-the-job practice sessions are used to refine interviewing skills. (Telephone numbers used in practice should be a random subset of the sampling pool so as not to bias the final sample.)

When a surveyor can afford to take this approach, it further serves to screen those interviewers who are likely to gather the best-quality data, especially from among a new group of interviewers. In fact, a final employment decision can be withheld until after each new interviewer has completed at least one practice session. Missing a scheduled practice session may also be an indication of the interviewer's potential unreliability.

In both practice sessions and actual work sessions it is the supervisor's responsibility to provide constant feedback to interviewers about all aspects of their work. This is done by checking completions immediately as they occur, reviewing call-sheets that have not led to completions, and spending as much time as possible listening in on ongoing interviewing. Because this is very demanding work for a supervisor, a maximum of 10 interviewers should be employed for every one supervisor. During on-the-job practice sessions and in the early stages of a survey, even this ratio is high, so it is preferable to use more than one supervisor per session until most problems have been worked out.

Chapter 6 addresses in detail the role of supervisors before, during, and after interviewing sessions. Here it is sufficient to note that the rapport that supervisors develop with interviewers will have a great effect on the quality of data produced for a survey. There must be constant feedback, both verbal and written, from supervisors to interviewers, especially during the early part of a survey's field period, when on-the-job training is most critical. This should be done tactfully, never embarrassing an interviewer in the presence of other interviewers.

After each practice session supervisors and the field director should review the ability of new interviewers and make a decision as to whether or not to continue a person on a particular survey. Periodic reviews of interviewer performance should continue throughout the field period. Whenever necessary, supervisors or the field director should arrange for an interviewer who is not meeting standards to discuss needed improvements.

Theoretically on-the-job training never stops. It remains the supervisor's responsibility to monitor the quality of interviewing and thus to provide feedback to interviewers. When this is done by skilled, conscientious supervisors a group of highly skilled interviewers will result, one whose energetic processing of call-sheets and questionnaires does not bias or otherwise compromise the quality of the survey data.

EXERCISES

1. Produce a display ad for hiring interviewers at a telephone survey organization. Include graphics in the display.

2. Summarize the differences between conducting a telephone survey with paid interviewers versus conducting it with unpaid volunteers.

3. Write the dialogue of a scenario illustrating the possible exchange between a respondent who is very reluctant to participate in a survey and a highly persuasive (but polite) interviewer.

4. In outline form, plan a training session that would include 20 new (paid) interviewers and 20 previously employed interviewers. Indicate the time (in minutes) you would allocate to each part of the session.

5. As an in-class project, have class members assemble in small groups and practice the use of a telephone survey questionnaire via role-playing.

6

SUPERVISION II: STRUCTURING SUPERVISORY WORK

The quality of data that are gathered in a telephone survey is dependent on the quality of supervision that is instituted over the data collection process. Supervisory personnel have many tasks that must be performed apart from the time spent supervising ongoing interviews. This chapter reviews those other tasks and also includes a detailed discussion of the role of supervisory personnel during interviewing sessions.

The opportunity afforded by telephone surveys for intensive supervision over the entire survey process has been stressed throughout this text. Chapter 3 explained how a highly routinized system for processing the telephone numbers in a sampling pool may be structured. The importance of supervisory personnel, in particular the person who will control the sampling pool, was mentioned. Chapter 5 explained the role of the trainer in interviewer training sessions and the role of supervisors in continued on-the-job training. Mention was also made throughout Chapter 5 that interviewers should be aware of the responsibilities of supervisors in monitoring the interviewing session.

The present chapter focuses on other supervisory responsibilities throughout the telephone surveying process, and also provides further elaboration on some of the supervisory tasks that were discussed in Chapters 3 and 5. It touches upon the role of the survey's field director, the role of interviewing session supervisors, and other tasks that should be performed to provide a smooth-flowing telephone survey operation.

If it is not already obvious to the reader, it is quite possible that one person could assume *all* (or at least several) of the supervisory responsibilities for a telephone survey. For example, for the past six years I have taught a two-week unit on public opinion polling to undergraduates in a senior-level journalism class three times an academic year. As part of this unit the class participates as interviewers in an RDD telephone survey (final sample size of about 400-450 completions) using a systematic selection of respondents within households with up to three call-backs for hard-to-reach respondents. The questionnaire averages about 15-20 closed-ended items and takes only a few minutes to administer. Within a 10-day period I generate the sampling pool, develop the questionnaire, train the student interviewers, schedule and set up each interviewing session, supervise all interviewing, control the processing of the sampling pool, edit and key the data, and perform a fairly robust set of statistical analyses that are reported back to the class.

Although most users of this text are unlikely to have to assume all these responsibilities for a telephone survey, other users may need to assume even more. For example, a graduate student who is using a telephone survey to gather data for a thesis may not only have to perform the equivalent of all the supervisory tasks but may also have to conduct all of the interviewing.

STAFFING AND SCHEDULING INTERVIEWING SESSIONS

There are many duties for which supervisory personnel are responsible at times when no interviewing is taking place. In fact, if these duties were not performed, interviewing would not be possible or, at minimum, would be highly disorganized. The first of these responsibilities has to do with staffing and scheduling interviewers. Most of the discussion presented in this section concerning staffing assumes that interviewers will be paid for their work, but some of the considerations also apply to interviewers who are unpaid.

Staffing

In large survey organizations there will be a field director who assumes responsibility for hiring and staffing interviewers. In other instances someone in a supervisory capacity will take this on. As mentioned earlier, one can attract high-caliber interviewers if the wage is good. To be competitive in an urban area, I recommend that interviewers be paid in a way that allows them to earn, on average, about twice the minimum wage; in 1987 this would be about $7 per hour.

To determine how many interviewers will be needed to staff the survey's field period, one must take into account

(1) how productive each interviewer is likely to be during each work session;
(2) the number of times each interviewer will work per week;
(3) the average number of interviewers who will work per session;
(4) the number of interviewing sessions that will be held each week; and
(5) the total number of completions that are needed.

For example, if a survey used RDD sampling and the questionnaire took about 15 minutes to administer, interviewers might be expected to produce two completions per hour, or eight completions in a four-hour work session. If there were six work sessions scheduled each week with 10 telephones available for interviewing, then about 480 completions could be expected per week. Depending on the number of times interviewers worked each week, one could estimate how many interviewers would be needed to keep telephones fully staffed. The greater the total number of completions needed for the survey (i.e., the longer the field period), the more likely one would need to inflate the number of interviewers hired to allow for interviewer attrition.

If, in this example, the desired number of completions was 2,400, approximately five weeks of interviewing would be needed at full staff. If interviewers worked, on average, three sessions per week, then each interviewer over the five-week field period would be expected to produce about 120 completions (i.e., eight completions per session multiplied by three sessions per week multiplied by five weeks). Strictly speaking, the survey would require 20 interviewers to complete the 2,400 completions. It would be prudent to hire and train upwards of 25-30 interviewers to allow for interviewer attrition.

The best place to advertise for high-caliber interviewers is likely to be on or near college and university campuses. This will attract students, spouses of students and employees, and residents of the communities in which these institutions are located. Although students often make good interviewers, a common disadvantage to employing them is the unreliability of their attendance due to their academic commitments. Thus it is strongly recommended that interviewers not be hired exclusively from the student population if surveys are to be completed within the shortest possible (most cost-effective) field period.

As mentioned in Chapter 5, one of the most important attributes for making a hiring decision is an interviewer's telephone presence. Therefore, the person doing the hiring should interview applicants via telephone and rate the applicant's voice and style of speaking along dimensions deemed relevant to good telephone interviewing. These would include pleasantness, clarity, shyness, volume, intelligence, and maturity. To facilitate this rating, the application form should ask some open-ended questions that may not elicit answers that are directly relevant to the hiring decision but will get the applicant to talk.

Scheduling

After preliminary staffing decisions have been made and training has been completed, scheduling must be finalized. For surveys of the general public, evenings and weekend afternoons are the best time to reach most potential respondents. Every sampling area has its own idiosyncratic patterns of residents not being home, but people are generally more likely to be available in the evening and during the daytime on weekends. Except in areas where many people attend church meetings on Sunday evenings, we consistently have found Sunday evenings to be the most productive time for interviewing.

If four-hour interviewing sessions are planned, then 5:00-9:00 p.m. or 5:30-9:30 p.m. is recommended for evening sessions. Even though this overlaps with the dinner hour, skilled interviewers should have no problem arranging a call-back at a more convenient time. Obviously, if a survey is sampling across time zones, interviewing hours should be adjusted accordingly.

Monday through Thursday evenings normally have constant levels of productivity, with the exception of Mondays during the fall months, when a proportion of the public seems not to want to be bothered when professional football is on television. Friday and Saturday evenings are the least productive because they are the times when most social entertaining is done. (Similarly, interviewers and supervisors are least likely to want to work on these evenings.)

Saturday daytime, from 10:00 a.m. to 6:00 p.m. is a fairly productive time for interviewing in most areas, despite the fact that call-backs are more likely because designated respondents are often doing weekend chores and running errands. During certain times of the year, however, Saturday and Sunday afternoons will show a decrease in productivity, especially among male respondents, many of whom might be watching televised sports events.

There will be other occasions on which normal evening sessions should be canceled because of some television special that is likely to be watched by a substantial proportion of the public. Not only will productivity be low at these times, but adamant refusals are more likely to be experienced than would occur had certain households been called on another occasion.

Depending on the time constraints for the length of the survey's field period, daytime interviewing during weekdays may be necessary. Afternoon hours, 1:00-5:00 p.m., are generally preferable to morning hours. Experience shows that interviewer productivity during weekday afternoons can be expected to be about 60%-80% that of evenings.

When daytime interviewing is scheduled for weekdays, these sessions can be quite helpful in cleaning RDD sampling pools of business and nonworking numbers. On the other hand, many more designated respondents will be unavailable because they are working. One advantage to including daytime sessions is that elderly respondents seem to be more alert. Furthermore, mothers who do not work outside the home seem more relaxed without their school-aged children and/or husbands around. When both males and females are to be chosen as designated respondents, a valid sample of males and of younger adults will not be achieved if only daytime sessions were to be scheduled.

With telephone surveys that sample some population other than the public at large, interviewing sessions will need to be scheduled at those times when respondents are most likely to be available. For example, a telephone survey of physicians or other professionals at their place of employment will most certainly need to concentrate interviewing during daytime hours on weekdays and allow for many call-backs. A telephone survey of high school students at their homes might concentrate interviewing between 3:00 and 7:00 p.m. on weekdays. Whatever the particular availability of the population being sampled, interviewing sessions should be targeted to those hours.

Seasonality should also be considered when scheduling a survey's field period. If there is any reason to believe that the focus of the survey may be confounded with the time of the year, explicit consideration should be made for its scheduling. For general population surveys, it is best not to collect data exclusively during summer months or in mid- to late December. Otherwise, one may end up with a somewhat biased sample, missing those persons most likely to be on vacation.

Once it has been determined when interviewing sessions will be scheduled, sufficient numbers of interviewers need to be slotted to keep available telephones fully staffed. If after a week of interviewing it is found that at least one telephone is regularly going unused because not all interviewers are attending their scheduled work sessions (and this is likely to happen due to the part-time nature of telephone interviewing), one alternative to consider is "overbooking" interviewers. For example, if 10 telephones are available, one may choose to schedule 11 interviewers for each session, knowing from experience that on most occasions at least one will not attend. This, of course, can create problems when all scheduled interviewers *do* appear. There are different ways this can be handled, including the possibility of paying the "extra" interviewer some compensation for not being able to interview (i.e., similar to what airlines are required to do with passengers who are "bumped").

Depending on how many telephones are used during interviewing sessions, it can be quite time consuming to schedule interviewers. It is recommended that a person with supervisory experience make these contacts so that judgment can be exercised on the likelihood that the contacted interviewer will, in fact, work those sessions he or she has agreed to. If attendance has been a problem for a specific interviewer, then a call to schedule work sessions can also serve as a warning about possible termination.

INTERVIEWING SESSION SETUP

Apart from the need to utilize a good system for staffing and scheduling interviewers, supervisory personnel also need to set up the centralized telephoning location on a daily basis. This must be done prior to the beginning of each work session and assumes that certain tasks have been completed since the end of the previous session of interviewing.

When interviewers arrive they should find the interviewing room arranged for them to begin interviewing. Their work stations should be well-lit, clean, and organized, with call-sheets, questionnaires, and pencils awaiting them. Ideally, each telephone will be positioned at its own carrel or booth to "enclose" interviewers in their own environments. But if this type of furniture is not available, telephones can be located at tables, none of which should have interviewers facing each other.

Before the interviewing room can be fully set up, call-sheets from the previous work session must be sorted according to their most recent disposition. Telephone numbers that are still active (e.g., specific call-back, ring-no-answer, busy, respondent not home, etc.) are then interspersed with a small number of new (untried) call-sheets. A sufficient amount of call-sheets to keep interviewers busy for about half the work session should be placed at each work station.

It is best not to give interviewers too many call-sheets to start with; as they need more they can get these from the supervisor, thus signaling that they are making progress in dialing numbers. Another reason that it is preferable to have supervisors control the flow of call-sheets prior to and during work sessions is that interviewers, if allowed to choose for themselves, will often display idiosyncratic behaviors that may bias sampling. For example, some interviewers prefer call-sheets that have not been tried; others prefer sheets in which the designated respondent has already been chosen. Furthermore, when interviewers are required to approach the supervisor for more call-sheets, it serves as an additional check on whether they are processing numbers too quickly or too slowly.

With experience, the person responsible for setting up the work sessions will learn how many call-sheets the average interviewer can be expected to process during the first half of the work session. This will depend on the length of the questionnaire and the efficiency of the sampling pool. With longer questionnaires, proportionally more of an interviewer's time will be spent interviewing rather than dialing numbers, thus fewer call-sheets will be processed. In contrast, with a shorter questionnaire and a less efficient sampling pool, more of interviewers' time will be spent cleaning the sample of nonworking and other ineligible telephone numbers; thus more call-sheets will be processed.

In addition to assigning call-sheets to each work station, questionnaires and sharpened pencils should also be placed there. It is good practice to place fewer questionnaires at each work station than the number that interviewers, on average, will complete in the entire work session. Psychologically this will reinforce for interviewers that they have made progress during the work session because they have used up all the questionnaires at their work stations. They can then get more new questionnaires from some centralized location in the interviewing room.

Depending on the type of equipment used for telephoning, a different amount of cleaning will be required prior to each work session. At minimum, each work station (including the chair) should be dusted prior to interviewers' arrival. If telephones have individualized headsets, then interviewers can be expected to keep earpieces clean. (The microphone on most types of headsets does not come in contact with an interviewer's mouth and should only occasionally need cleaning.) But if standard telephone receivers are used, the external surface of the mouth-piece and the earpiece of each receiver must be cleaned, preferably with alcohol or some other nontoxic solvent, prior to each session. At least once a week each receiver should be disassembled and cleaned from the inside.

Cleanliness in the work setting is not merely a courtesy to inter-viewers, it serves to reinforce order. Even more important, it helps to keep interviewers healthy. Given the importance of the interviewer's voice in telephone surveys, colds and other respiratory infections greatly impair their ability to do good interviewing. Given that unreliable attendance is often a problem with part-time telephone interviewers, it behooves the organization or person conducting the survey not to contribute to interviewers' potential health problems. Cleaning tele-phone receivers before each work session is one way to lessen the likelihood that colds and infection will spread.

A final aspect of preparing the interviewing room prior to each work session is the inclusion of interviewer-specific information in their work folders. There should be a file cabinet or set of mailboxes near where interviewing occurs that contains a separate folder for each interviewer. After interviewers sign in, they retrieve these folders to review any notes or other information before beginning to call. With such a system, supervisory personnel can assign partial questionnaires to specific interviewers for reprocessing. Memos to all interviewers can be put in folders, as can notes about specific problems from the previous time an interviewer worked. If something more serious needs to be discussed with an interviewer prior to her or his continuing to interview, the supervisor can place a note in the folder requesting the interviewer to see the supervisor before starting to interview.

If interviewers arrive at a centralized location that looks organized, this will help convey an expectancy of the professional quality of interviewing that is desired of them. Supervisory personnel will not only do a more uniform job of setting up the work sessions, but by relieving interviewers of these types of tasks it allows them to concentrate on what they were hired to do: good quality interviewing, not "housekeeping."

SUPERVISING INTERVIEWING SESSIONS

As exhausting as telephone interviewing can be, the demands on the supervisor of an interviewing session can be even greater. It is this person's responsibility to ensure the integrity of sampling and the quality of the data that are collected. For these reasons energetic and skilled individuals should be employed in supervisory positions and paid accordingly—approximately three times the minimum wage, which in 1987 is about $10 per hour.

Experience has shown that those persons who have had at least some graduate school education in the social sciences often have the qualities of good supervisors: They are generally intelligent, willing to work hard in support of quality data collection, and usually have a good appreciation of research and the role of sampling and interviewing within that broader endeavor.

In general, considering both costs and data quality, an optimal ratio should be one supervisor for every eight to 10 experienced interviewers. When a supervisor is responsible for more than 10 interviewers, the time demands become so intense that it is difficult for quality supervision to occur. On the other hand, it is neither cost-effective nor often necessary to limit the number of interviewers for which a supervisor is responsible to fewer than eight. With new interviewers or at the start of a survey's field period, however, it is prudent to maintain closer to a 5:1 ratio (i.e., temporarily use two supervisors for every 10 interviewers).

For a survey in which several supervisors are employed, it is the responsibility of the person serving in the capacity of field director to supervise the supervisors. This includes their hiring, their training, and the constant review of their on-the-job performance. Supervisors should know that the field director may appear at an interviewing session unannounced to observe how the session is progressing; that is, to assess how well the supervisor is executing her or his responsibilities. These responsibilities are addressed below.

Validating Completions

As mentioned in Chapter 5, upon completion of an interview each interviewer should be instructed to check over the questionnaire quickly yet carefully and then *immediately* turn it in to the supervisor. The supervisor, in turn, should inspect the entire questionnaire, item by item, to validate that answers were recorded for all items asked, all skip patterns were properly followed, and the answers to all open-ended questions are written legibly. To be able to do this accurately *and* quickly, the supervisor must be completely familiar with the questionnaire.

Unless the supervisor is involved in the resolution of some problem or answering a question for an interviewer, validation of completions should be the supervisor's *first* priority. The purpose of this intensive level of supervision is to catch problems as soon as they occur. The supervisor can then immediately discuss the resolution of the problem with the interviewer before it happens again. Many times a problem can be resolved without the interviewer having to call the respondent back. In those instances in which information is missing entirely, the supervisor should instruct the interviewer to call the respondent back immediately to gather the missing data, as the respondent is quite likely to still be available, having hung up only a few minutes earlier.

Once a questionnaire has been validated by the supervisor as being properly completed, the supervisor should initial the attached call-sheet to allow for easy identification of who did the validation. This is one of the ways in which supervisory personnel are held accountable. The field director should occasionally revalidate completions to check the attentiveness of supervisors. Furthermore, when questionnaires are later edited by the survey sponsor or whoever is checking the questionnaire before it is key-punched, problems that are detected can easily be traced back to the supervisor on duty during the interviewing session in which the completion occurred.

The manner in which a supervisor gives feedback to interviewers should be timely and direct, yet tactful. An interviewer should never be made to feel embarrassed by a supervisor in front of other interviewers. This can be avoided if the supervisor writes a note to the interviewer either explaining a minor problem or requesting to speak with the interviewer before the interviewer goes on to another interview. In the extreme, supervisors must have the discretion to ask an interviewer to stop interviewing for the remainder of a work session if a problem has occurred that the interviewer appears unable or unwilling to correct.

Although it is unreasonable to expect perfection on the part of interviewers and supervisors, a supervisor who concentrates while validating questionnaires should allow very few interviewing mistakes to slip past. Similarly, when interviewers recognize that their ongoing work is carefully monitored it encourages their attentiveness to conducting interviews.

Listening to Ongoing Interviews

Whenever possible, a centralized bank of telephones should be installed with equipment that allows the supervisor's telephone to monitor all interviewers' lines. There are special telephones that can monitor an ongoing interview without the interviewer or respondent being aware of it, but this can also been done if the supervisor's desk is equipped with a regular telephone that ties into each access line used by interviewers. In this latter case the supervisor disconnects the mouth-piece before cutting into the line. When this happens the interviewer (but usually not the respondent) will be aware that the supervisor is listening. Although this may create some disadvantages (e.g., a slight drop in volume on the line), one advantage is the fact that interviewers are certain that the quality of their interviewing is being assessed.

Supervisors need not listen to complete interviews but should spread their listening, a few minutes at a time, across all interviewers, concentrating more frequently and at longer intervals on less experienced ones. All aspects of interviewer-respondent contact should be monitored: This includes the interviewer's use of the introduction, the selection procedure, fallback statements, and the questionnaire itself.

Supervisors should pay special attention to ways in which interviewers probe for further clarification of ambiguous or irrelevant responses. They also need to pay close attention to anything the interviewer may be saying or doing that might reinforce certain response patterns that may bias the data. For example, interviewers should never express their own opinions, even when a respondent asks them, "What do you think?" Nor should interviewers fall into the unconscious habit of saying things like "that's too bad", or "I'm glad to hear that."

When the telephone system that is used for interviewing does not allow a supervisor to listen on interviewers' access lines, the supervisor should frequently walk around the interviewing room, stopping behind each interviewer to listen for a while to the interviewer's part of the conversation. Anyone who has experience with telephone interviewing knows that it is very difficult to "fake" an interview successfully if an experienced supervisor is within listening distance and paying attention to what the interviewer is doing. From experience, a supervisor should be able to detect a bad interview by its pacing and the inconsistency of the apparent responses.

Thus although it is certainly preferable to have a telephone system that allows supervisors to listen directly to ongoing interviews, this aspect of the supervisor's responsibilities should occur regardless of the availibility of monitoring equipment.

Listening to ongoing interviewing should be more intense in the early stages of the field period and with new interviewers; this is why it was suggested that there are occasions on which two supervisors are preferred for every 10 interviewers, rather than a 10:1 ratio. Monitoring should not be stopped in later stages of the field period, nor should supervisors avoid listening to experienced interviewers. Rather, they must show common sense in how they allocate their listening time, scheduling it as second in importance to the immediate validation of completions.

Monitoring Call-Sheet Dispositions

It is also the supervisor's responsibility to oversee the processing of call-sheets *during* the interviewing session. Supervisors should occasionally check the manner in which refusals and partials are being recorded by interviewers, as well as how they are using all disposition codes. Again, the supervisor should concentrate this attention on new interviewers.

Another supervisory responsibility regarding call-sheets concerns the recycling of certain call-sheets during the interviewing session. From previous sessions certain call-sheets may need to be redialed at a particular time or should be given to a particular interviewer. The supervisor should see that these call-sheets get to the right interviewer at the right time. Similarly, there are times when one interviewer will lack the confidence to call back a respondent from the interviewer's previous session to try to complete a partial. The supervisor should discuss this reluctance with the original interviewer and then decide whether to reassign the partial to another interviewer.

Solving Problems and Answering Questions

At all times during interviewing sessions supervisors must be trouble-shooters. They must know how to answer interviewers' questions, anticipate and solve problems, and generally be ready to deal with the unexpected. Sometimes interpersonal tensions between interviewers will need to be defused. Other times interviewers may become too chatty, thus taking away from their productivity. Occasionally a supervisor may need to speak with an irate or upset respondent to apologize for some mistake on the part of an interviewer, or to resolve some uncertainty that the interviewer cannot explain, or simply to listen courteously to a respondent who requests to talk to a supervisor.

When the Sponsor Visits

A final issue regarding the work of supervisors while interviewing is taking place has to do with those work sessions in which the survey's sponsor is in attendance as an observer. Sponsors have good reason to want to observe the sessions in which their data are being gathered. A sponsor pays for the survey and thus is clearly justified to want firsthand evidence of how interviewers are using the questionnaire and what respondents are saying.

Often, however, a sponsor has unrealistic expectations about the enthusiasm that respondents display while participating in telephone surveys. The naive sponsor presumes that her or his questionnaire will be interesting and important to all respondents and thus automatically assumes it to be the fault of interviewers if some respondents sound somewhat unfocused and/or uninterested while responding.

With this and other problems created by a sponsor observing ongoing interviewing sessions, the supervisor must be ready to listen to the concerns of the sponsor but should not deviate from standard survey procedures until the field director has changed policy. At no time should supervisors argue with survey sponsors. Rather, the sponsor should be asked to discuss any concerns with the field director, who will then inform supervisors of any changes that are warranted.

VERIFYING COMPLETED INTERVIEWS

An additional supervisory duty is associated with the *verification* of completed surveys. In addition to the supervisor's validation of each completion during the interviewing session, a survey can be planned to include verification of some percentage of all completed interviews. Verification of completions requires a supervisory-level person to recontact the respondent to verify that the interview took place and to verify some of the answers recorded by the interviewer.

If a telephone survey employs a highly rigorous monitoring of ongoing interviewing as described in this chapter, verifying completions may be viewed as optional. Verification is especially recommended, however, with new interviewers and at the beginning of a survey's field period. Psychologically it is a good idea for interviewers to know that verification occurs, but it is not necessary for them to know how many of their completions are actually verified.

Any completion that does not verify is cause for concern. It does not necessarily mean that the interview was done improperly (e.g., there are times when respondents will unaccountably be reluctant to admit they participated in a survey), but it signals the need to be vigilant in checking the work of a particular interviewer.

CONCLUSION

As Fowler (1984) observed, far too little attention has been paid by survey professionals to sources of error associated with the human part of survey data collection. As should be clear from this chapter, and from the text as a whole, the quality of the sampling that occurs and the data that are gathered in a telephone survey are highly correlated with the quality of the supervision that is implemented.

Many survey organizations, especially commercial ones, appear unwilling to institute a system that stresses *and* rewards quality telephone interviewing and supervision. Unfortunately, the practice (inadvertent though it may be) of underutilizing the opportunities that telephone surveys provide for a rigorous control of data collection is likely to continue until survey sponsors recognize the need to demand higher quality for their money.

Throughout this text the procedures that have been explained assume that a surveyor would like to gather the highest-quality data possible at a reasonable cost. As with many things, cutting telephone survey costs most often means cutting quality. In many instances poor-quality interviewing and inadequate supervision may even be more expensive than top-quality work, especially when the quality is so poor as to invalidate the data that have been gathered. Simply stated, money spent to gather poor-quality survey data is money wasted.

EXERCISES

1. Develop an information form for use by a field director to screen applicants, via telephone, for positions as telephone interviewers.

2. Calculate the number of interviewing sessions to schedule per week and the number of interviewers to employ for the following survey that must be completed in three weeks: 1,500 completions are required; interviewers will average about 1.5 completions per hour; interviewing sessions will last three hours each; there are eight telephones in the centralized interviewing room; and interviewers will work an average of four sessions per week.

3. Write a work description for a newly hired supervisor explaining the supervisory duties that are expected *during* an interviewing session. Limit the narrative to 300 words or less.

4. Develop a one-page form that could be used to verify completed interviews.

APPENDIX A

AN SPSS PROGRAM FOR GENERATING
RDD SAMPLING POOLS

For those persons who do not already have a computer program that will generate an RDD sampling pool, this appendix contains a listing of a four-step SPSS program that should be fairly easy to use by those familiar with SPSS. The program, as listed here, was written by Robert K. LeBailly and myself (LeBaily & Lavrakas, 1981) to run on a Cyber at Northwestern University prior to the introduction of SPSS-X. Those with access to, and preference for, SPSSX will need to modify the statements to conform to X's protocol.

As written and documented Step 1 assumes the user has all three possible types of information about telephone prefixes in the sampling area. These include (1) an exhaustive listing of prefixes; (2) the number of residential access lines assigned to each prefix, or at least a fairly precise estimate of this; and (3) ranges of vacuous or nonoperative banks of suffixes for each prefix. With this information the sampling pool that is generated will be stratified by prefixes, making it much more efficient from the standpoint of interviewer processing time than a simple (unstratified) RDD sampling pool. As discussed in Chapter 2, unless information about the number of access lines per prefix and/or vacuous banks of suffixes is available for *every* prefix, Step 1 will need further modification because partial information cannot be used without causing a probable bias in the sampling pool.

The output from each step is used as input for the next step. Step 1 generates a preliminary group of prefixes totaling the approximate number that is anticipated will be needed for sampling. Step 2 assigns a random four-digit suffix to each prefix within its operating range of suffixes. Step 3 cleans the preliminary sampling pool of duplicates and, if desired, of numbers that end in multiple zeros and sorts the remaining cases in random order. Step 4 is a report generator for printing multiple call-sheets, each with a unique random telephone number for interviewers to process.

STEP 1

In the following listing COMMENT statements provide adequate documentation for those familiar with SPSS. The possible exception is the explanation of the variable, RANGEPCT. This variable, which is entered as data by the user, represents the proportion of a prefix's operating range that is covered by a bank of consecutive suffixes. For example, if a prefix operated from 1000-1899, 3000-4999, and 7000-9499, then there would be 900 plus 2,000 plus 2,500, or a total operating range of 5,400 suffixes. The 1000-1899 bank would account for 16.67% of the total operating range of suffixes (i.e., 900/5400 = .1667); similarly, 37.04% would be accounted for by the 3000-4999 bank, as would 46.30% by the 7000-9499 bank. Whenever there is a single range of consecutive suffixes associated with a prefix, regardless of its length, the RANGEPCT variable takes on a value of 1.0 for that prefix.

```
RUN NAME         GENERATE RDD SAMPLING POOL, STEP 1
COMMENT          AT STEP 1 A CASE IS READ IN FOR EACH UNIQUE SUFFIX RANGE.
                 A PREFIX WITH A SINGLE SUFFIX RANGE WILL BE REPRESENTED BY
                 ONE CASE. A PREFIX WITH THREE SUFFIX RANGES WILL BE REPRESENTED
                 BY THREE CASES.
COMMENT          DESCRIPTION OF INPUT DATA VARIABLES:
                 PREFIX    THE FIRST 3 DIGITS OF A TELEPHONE NUMBER
                 NPHPRE    THE TOTAL NUMBER OF RESIDENTIAL ACCESS LINES IN THE
                           PREFIX (ALL SUFFIX RANGES FOR THAT PREFIX)
                 LORANGE   THE LOWEST SUFFIX (LAST FOUR DIGITS OF TELEPHONE
                           NUMBER) IN THE CURRENT SUFFIX RANGE
                 HIRANGE   THE HIGHEST SUFFIX IN THE CURRENT SUFFIX RANGE
                 RANGEPCT  THE PROPORTION OF THE ENTIRE PREFIX RANGE COVERED
                           BY THE CURRENT SUFFIX RANGE
VARIABLE LIST    PREFIX NPHPRE LORANGE HIRANGE RANGEPCT
INPUT FORMAT     FREEFIELD
COMMENT          NPHPOP IS THE NUMBER OF ACCESS LINES IN THE POPULATION
COMPUTE          NPHPOP= [value entered by user]
COMMENT          NSAMPLE IS THE ESTIMATED SIZE OF THE FINAL SAMPLING POOL
COMPUTE          NSAMPLE= [value entered by user]
COMMENT          NRANGE IS THE COMPUTED SIZE OF THE SAMPLING POOL ASSOCIATED
                 WITH A PARTICULAR SUFFIX RANGE
COMPUTE          NRANGE=RANGEPCT*(NPHPRE/NPNPOP)*NSAMPLE
WEIGHT           NRANGE
WRITE CASES      (F3.0,2F6.0) PREFIX LORANGE HIRANGE
READ INPUT DATA
FINISH
```

STEP 2

The output from Step 1 is a series of prefix replicates generated by the weight statement. It is the responsibility of the individual user to include the proper system statements unique to the user's computer operating environment to make certain the output from the WRITE CASES procedure is saved. In Step 2 each prefix replicate receives a random four-digit suffix within the various ranges of its operating banks of suffixes.

```
RUN NAME         GENERATE RDD SAMPLING POOL, STEP 2
COMMENT          INPUT DATA IS FROM THE WRITE CASES OF STEP 1. EACH CASE IN
                 STEP 1 HAS BEEN REPLICATED NRANGE TIMES.
```

```
DATA LIST       PREFIX 1-3 LORANGE 6-9 HIRANGE 12-15
COMMMENT        GENERATE A RANDOM SUFFIX BETWEEN LORANGE AND HIRANGE
SEED            PRINT
COMPUTE         RANGE=(HIRANGE-LORANGE)+1
COMPUTE         SUFFIX=TRUNC(UNIFORM(RANGE))+LORANGE
COMMMENT        COMPUTE PHONE# -- THE SEVEN DIGIT TELEPHONE NUMBER
COMPUTE         PHONE#=PREFIX*(10000)+SUFFIX
TASK NAME       DISTRIBUTION OF PREFIXES WITH POSSIBLE DUPLICATE SUFFIXES
FREQUENCIES     GENERAL=PREFIX
SORT CASES      PHONE#
KEEP VARS       PREFIX SUFFIX PHONE#
SAVE FILE       TEMP SPSS FILE CREATED IN STEP 2 WITH POSSIBLE DUPLICATES
FINISH
```

STEP 3

The output that has been saved from Step 2 is then read as input for Step 3. As listed here, Step 3 cleans the sample of duplicate telephone numbers and of numbers that end in multiple zeros. If the surveyor prefers, this final sequence can be omitted, which will then allow such numbers to be cleaned by interviewers' processing of the sampling pool.

```
RUN NAME        GENERATE RDD SAMPLING POOL, STEP 3
GET FILE        TEMP
COMMENT         ELIMINATE DUPLICATE TELEPHONE NUMBERS
COMPUTE         LAGPHONE=LAG(PHONE#)
SELECT IF       (PHONE# NE LAGPHONE)
COMMENT         ELIMINATE NUMBERS ENDING WITH MULTIPLE ZEROS
COMPUTE         END=SUFFIX-(TRUNC(SUFFIX/100)*100)
SELECT IF       (END NE 0)
COMMENT         REORDER REMAINING NUMBERS RANDOMLY
COMPUTE         RANDOM=UNIFORM(1)
SORT CASES      RANDOM
TASK NAME       FREQUENCY OF PREFIXES IN FINAL RDD SAMPLING POOL
FREQUENCIES     GENERAL=PREFIX
KEEP VARS       PREFIX SUFFIX
SAVE FILE       PHONE FINAL RDD SAMPLING POOL
FINISH
```

STEP 4

This final step uses SPSS's report generator to print as many call-sheets as are needed at any one time from the sampling pool. Each call-sheet is printed with one of the RDD telephone numbers in the sampling pool. Call-sheets are generated in the random order they were sorted at the end of Step 3. The user can control the number of call-sheets that are printed by specifying the desired SEQNUM range in a SELECT IF statement (i.e., if the user wants the first 500 numbers printed, then the SELECT IF statement would be written as shown below). For the next 500 numbers the user would simply change the operative values in the SELECT IF statement to print those with SEQNUM ranging from 501-1000.

```
RUN NAME        PRINT CALL-SHEETS USING FINAL RDD SAMPLING POOL, STEP 4
GET FILE        PHONE
COMPUTE         SEQ#=SEQNUM
SELECT IF       (SEQNUM GE 1 AND SEQNUM LE 500)      [user has option here]
COMMENT         CREATE FOUR ALPHA VARIABLES (SUF1-SUF4) EQUIVALENT TO THE
                FOUR DIGITS IN THE NUMERIC VARIABLE -- SUFFIX -- SO THAT
                REPORT GENERATOR WILL PRINT LEADING ZEROS IN SUFFIXES, E.G.,
                0123 AND 0075.
COMPUTE         REMAINS=SUFFIX
DO REPEAT       A=SUF1 SUF2 SUF3/B=1000 100 10/
COMPUTE         A=TRUNC(REMAINS/B)
COMPUTE         REMAINS=REMAINS-(A*B)
END REPEAT
COMPUTE         SUF4=REMAINS
RECODE          SUF1 SUF2 SUF3 SUF4 (0='0')(1='1')(2='2')(3='3')(4='4')(5='5')
                (6='6')(7='7')(8='8')(9='9')
PRINT FORMATS   SUF1 SUF2 SUF3 SUF4 (A)
REPORT          FORMAT=NOLIST,MARGINS(9,71),BRKSPACE(6),LENGTH(3,12)
                CHDSPACE(2)/
                STRING=PHONE#(PREFIX(3)'-'SUF1(1) SUF2(1) SUF3(1) SUF4(1))/
                VARS=SEQ# ' ' (5)/
                BREAK=CALL# 'PHONE NUMBER' (14) (PAGE)/
                SUMMARY=MEAN 'SEQUENCE #:' (SEQ#(0))/
                CHEAD='CALL-SHEET: [user added title] '/
                LHEAD=')DATE'/
                RHEAD='PAGE )PAGE'/
                LFOOT=
```

'CONTACT ATTEMPTS	QUESTIONNAIRE NO.		[1-4]'
		-- -- -- --'
' '			
' ' DATE	TIME	DISP.	INT. ID'
' '			
' '			
' 1 ___ / ___ / ___	___ : '		
' __ __ __ __ __ __	__ __ __ __	__ __	__ --'
' '			
' '			
' 2 ___ / ___ / ___	___ : '		
' __ __ __ __ __ __	__ __ __ __	__ __	__ --'
' '			
' '			
' 3 ___ / ___ / ___	___ : '		
' __ __ __ __ __ __	__ __ __ __	__ __	__ --'
' '			
' '			

```
'  4          /      /                          : '
'        -- --    -- --   -- --        -- --   -- --     -- --       -- -- '
' '
' '
'  5          /      /                          : '
'        -- --    -- --   -- --        -- --   -- --     -- --       -- -- '
' '
' '
'  6          /      /                          : '
'        -- --    -- --   -- --        -- --   -- --     -- --       -- -- '
' '
' '
' '
' '
'                              NOTES '
' '
' '
'_____'
' '
' '
'_____'
' '
' '
'_____'
' '
' '
'_____'
' '
' '
'_____'
```

As shown above, a blank space is provided for a four-digit questionnaire number to be coded on the call-sheet for those that yield completed interviews. Formatting for the keying of this ID number in columns 1-4 is also provided. Other information can be keyed from the call-sheet (e.g., the number of times a call-sheet was processed, the final disposition code, and the interviewer who processed the sheet the final time). Formatting codes for keying these data would then need to be added to this SPSS report generator.

APPENDIX B

A NOTE ON QUESTIONNAIRE FORMATTING

A good deal has been written regarding the development and refinement of questionnaire items. Almost all of this has been done by those experienced with self-administered questionniares and face-to-face interviewing. Few authors have addressed the issue of item construction specifically for telephone surveys. Unfortunately, this text cannot properly cover it either. Suffice to say that telephone surveys are more limited in the types, length, and complexity of items that can reliably be asked of respondents. Whenever new items are planned for inclusion in a telephone survey questionnaire (i.e., items that have not been used before), they should be pilot tested prior to the start of actual interviewing.

Regardless of how one assembles a set of items, orders them, and finalizes the questionnaire, a critical rule to remember is that the interviewer is the *primary user* of the questionnaire. This means that the form or layout of items within a questionnaire should be planned with the interviewer first in mind. It should be the expressed purpose of the questionnaire format to relieve the interviewer of as much burden as possible. Items must be printed in a way that makes their use as easy as possible. Items should be easy to read *and* it should be easy to record an answer.

Some surveyors are "penny wise and pound foolish" when it comes to formatting a questionnaire. Saving money at this point should be a minor consideration when weighed against the need to provide interviewers with the best possible routine with which to work. In some extreme instances surveyors short-sightedly choose to provide interviewers with one copy of the question-naire and expect them to record responses on a separate answer sheet. They reason that they can save printing and key-punching costs if answers are recorded by interviewers directly on optical scanning forms, for example. This is a big burden on telephone interviewers, who already have a difficult task without it being made more difficult by expecting them to work with an awkward routine.

The following are some suggestions for laying out a telephone survey questionnaire on paper.

NEVER CROWD A PAGE

For the convenience of interviewers, it is best to space items liberally. This includes an extra half-space between responses and double or triple spacing between items. A single item should always appear on the same page—never continue it to a following page. Whenever possible, a series of related items should also be printed on the same page.

FLOWING INTO RESPONSE CHOICES

Without compromising the convenience to interviewers, response choices to items can often "flow" from the beginning wording, as shown in Figure B.1. This type of formatting avoids retyping a set of responses and is easily used by interviewers familiar with this design, who simply follow the punctuation. Responses that are not read to respondents should be printed in all capital letters or italicized, as a reminder to interviewers. Not all questionnaire items will lend themselves to this type of formatting, but because of its parsimony it should be used whenever possible.

Figure B.1. Example of Telephone Survey Item Formatting

Q23. How safe do you feel or would you feel being out alone at night in your
     neighborhood? Would you say . . .

                    very safe, ... 4 [SKIP TO Q25]

                    somewhat safe, ... 3

                    somewhat unsafe, or. 2

                    very unsafe? 1

                    NEVER GO OUT 7

                    DON'T KNOW 9

Q24. Where in your neighborhood do you feel or would your feel most unsafe to
     be? [PROBE AMBIGUOUS OR MULTIPLE RESPONSES TO GET ONE EXACT LOCATION]

     _____

Q25. How satisfied are you with the quality of police services in your
     neighborhood? Are you . . .

                    very satisfied,. . . . . 4 [SKIP TO Q27]

                    somewhat satisfied,. 3

Figure B.1   Continued
_____

somewhat dissatisfied, or. . . . 2

very dissatisfied? 1

DON'T KNOW 9

Q26. What aspects of police services are you dissatisfied with?

_____

_____

_____

_____

CIRCLING PRECODED NUMERICAL CODES

Responses should be laid out so that interviewers circle a precoded number rather than placing a check mark in a blank. This causes no inconvenience to interviewers and greatly facilitates key-punching. Leader dots should be used (as shown in Figure B.1) from the printed response to its associated numerical code, so that interviewers' vision naturally follows to the proper number to circle. Finally, numerical codes should be printed in the same column down an entire page, not changing from item to item.

OPEN-ENDED ITEMS

When open-ended items are included in a questionnaire, the surveyor must decide *in advance* how detailed, and thus lengthy, an answer should be expected. Once this decision is made for each open-ended item, the appropriate number of double- or triple-spaced lines should be typed below the item on which interviewers can write (i.e., similar to ruled notebook paper), as shown in Figure B.1. space is left below open-ended items. First, it enhances legibility; second, it creates an expectancy for interviewers regarding the length of a response to elicit from respondents. For example, open-ended items with five ruled lines beneath will cue interviewers that a more detailed answer is expected than items having only two or three ruled lines.

NOTES TO INTERVIEWERS

Whenever a note or some form of instruction is printed to help interviewers with specific item or set of responses, it should be done in all capital letters or in italics. Establishing such a convention makes it easy for interviewers to distinguish what they are to read to a respondent from what is only a note or instructions to them and thus is not to be read. Figure B.1 also illustrates this distinction.

Whenever a set of instructions is especially important or complicated, a surveyor may want to print them within a box so that they stand out more. With word processors becoming more affordable, boldface print can also be considered for emphasizing reminders to interviewers.

SKIP PATTERNS

Surveyors differ in their opinions on how to format items that require interviewers to skip ahead to some other place in the questionnaire. My preference is for interviewers to be provided written instructions, not to expect them to follow leader arrows with their eyes. As shown in Figure B.1, interviewers simply follow the appropriate instructions associated with responses that require skips. If no message follows a response, the interviewer simply asks the next item.

With complicated skip patterns a surveyor may have to pilot test several versions of a page, or sequence of pages, before finding one that is most easily (and thus most accurately) used by interviewers. If interviewers are required to skip ahead several pages in the questionnaire, it is very useful to *color code* that page by printing it on paper stock other than white. For example, rather than print "SKIP TO PAGE 14," interviewers will find it easier to follow "SKIP TO BLUE," where page 14 is printed on blue stock. Depending on the need, several colored pages can be included within the same questionnaire.

MATRIX FORMAT

A final suggestion has to do with series of items that employ the same response choices, such as several questions in a row that ask if the respondent "agrees strongly, agrees somewhat, disagrees somewhat, or disagrees strongly." As a way of economizing on paper and at the same time providing a convenience to interviewers, an *item-response matrix* can be printed, such as that shown in Figure B.2.

Figure B.2. Example of Item-Response Matrix Formatting

```
Q27. Now I'm going to read you a list of crime-related problems that may exist
     in some parts of the city. For each one, I'd like you to indicate whether
     you think it's a big problem, some problem or basically no problem in your
     neighborhood.
                                   big        some        no       DON'T
                                 problem,  problem, or problem?    KNOW

     A. What about burglary? That
        is, someone breaking in
        or sneaking into homes to
        steal something? Is that
        a . . . [REPEAT RESPONSES] . . . 3 . . . . . 2 . . . . . 1 . . . . 9


     B. Vandalism, like kids
        breaking windows, writing
        on walls or things like that?. . 3 . . . . . 2 . . . . . 1 . . . . 9

     C. People using illegal drugs?. . . 3 . . . . . 2 . . . . . 1 . . . . 9

     D. People being robbed or having
        purses or wallets taken on
        the street?. . . . . . . . . . . 3 . . . . . 2 . . . . . 1 . . . . 9

     etc.
```

APPENDIX C

REVERSE DIRECTORIES FOR MAJOR CITIES

For those without access to a reverse directory at a local library, and for those who will need the convenience of having their own reverse directories, this appendix lists the companies that lease or sell reverse directories for major U.S. cities. It was assembled in 1985 and will become dated as time passes.

Atlanta, GA: Haines & Company, Inc.
8050 Freedom Avenue North West
North Canton, Ohio 44720
(216) 494-9111
City, Lease $129, Purchase $193.50
Suburban, Lease $133, Purchase $199.50

Baltimore, MD: Stewart Directories
304 West Chesapeake Avenue
Baltimore, Maryland 21204
(301) 823-4780
City, Lease $130

Boston, MA: Cole Publications
901 Bond Street
Lincoln, Nebraska 68521
(402) 475-4591
Central, Lease $184
North, Lease $126
South, Lease $126
West, Lease $126

Buffalo, NY: Haines & Company, Inc.
Lease $150, Purchase $225

Chicago, IL: Haines & Company, Inc.
City, Lease $295, Purchase $442.50
Far North, Lease $102, Purchase $153
Near North, Lease $130, Purchase $195
South, Lease $124, Purchase $186
West, Lease $143, Purchase $214.50

Cincinnati, OH: Haines & Company, Inc.
Lease $153, Purchase $229.50

Cleveland, OH: Haines & Company, Inc.
Lease $255, Purchase $382.50

Columbus, OH: Haines & Company, Inc.
                       Lease $139, Purchase $208.50

Dallas, TX: Cole Publications
                       Lease $195

Denver, CO: Cole Publications
                       Lease $170

Detroit, MI: Bressers Cross-Index Directory Co.
                       684 West Baltimore Street
                       Detroit, Michigan 48202
                       (313) 874-0570
                       Lease $226.60

El Paso, TX: Cole Publications
                       Lease $95

Houston, TX: Cole Publications
                       Lease $208

Indianapolis, IN: Haines & Company, Inc.
                       Lease $153, Purchase $229.50

Kansas City, MO: Cole Publications
                       Lease $125

Los Angeles, CA: Haines & Company, Inc.
                       City, Lease $155, Purchase $232.50
                       East, Lease $152, Purchase $228
                       North, Lease $155, Purchase $232.50
                       South, Lease $164, Purchase $256
                       West, Lease $122, Purchase $183

Louisville, KY: Woodward Directory Company
                       8609 Chellenham
                       Louisville, Kentucky 40222
                       (502) 425-1054
                       Purchase $190.50

Miami, FL: Bressers Cross-Index Directory Company
                       Lease $180.50

Milwaukee, WI: Bressers Cross-Index Directory Company
                       Lease $183

Minneapolis, MN: Cole Publications
                       Lease $140

Nashville, TN: City Publishing Company
                       118 South 8th Street
                       Independence, Kansas 67301
                       (316) 331-2650
                       Lease $84

New Orleans, LA:	Haines & Company, Inc.
	Lease $135, Purchase $202
New York City, NY:	Cole Publications
	Bronx, Lease $160
	Brooklyn, Lease $260
	Manhattan, Lease $315
	Queens, Lease $185
	Staten Island, Lease $100
Philadelphia, PA:	Cole Publications
	City, Lease $195
	Suburban, Lease $395
Phoenix, AZ:	Cole Publications
	Lease $178
Pittsburgh, PA:	Cole Publications
	Lease $164
Portland, OR:	Cole Publications
	Lease $118
St. Louis, MO:	Haines & Company, Inc.
	Lease $130, Purchase $195
Salt Lake City, UT:	Cole Publications
	Lease $140
San Antonio, TX:	Cole Publications
	Lease $180
San Francisco, CA:	Haines & Company, Inc.
	Lease $133, Purchase $199
Seattle, WA:	Cole Publications
	Lease $153
Tulsa, OK:	Cole Publications
	Lease $149
Washington, DC:	Haines & Company, Inc.
	Lease $116, Purchase $174
Canada, Montreal:	Cole Publications
	Lease $215
Toronto:	Metropolitan Cross-Reference Directory Limited
	2 Ripley Avenue
	Toronto, M6S 3N9,
	Ontario, Canada
	(416) 763-5515
	Lease $389, Purchase $576
Windsor:	Bressers Cross-Index Directory Company
	Lease $99

GLOSSARY

Access line. The telephone line in each household and nonresidence with telephone service that is associated with a distinct telephone number. In telephone surveys nontelephone households are those without any telephone access lines; those with more than one telephone number are referred to as having multiple access lines.

Add-a-digit. A technique for generating a sampling pool whereby "seed" numbers are typically chosen from a directory and then a fixed or random digit is added to each seed to form a number for the sampling pool. For example, if 869-5025 is chosen from a directory and fixed digit, 1, is added to all seeds, then 869-5026 is entered into the sampling pool.

Call-sheet. A separate piece of paper on which is printed each telephone number released from the sampling pool. Call-sheets provide the paper-and-pencil approach for controlling a sampling pool in the absence of CATI. Typical information recorded on the call-sheet includes the date, time, and disposition of each dialing along with the identification number of the interviewer who made each dialing and any relevant notes.

CATI. Computer-assisted telephone interviewing refers to those telephone survey operations that have interviewing performed with a computer terminal instead of a paper-and-pencil approach. These systems typically use the computers to form and control the sampling pool, prompt interviewers with the introductory spiel and selection procedure, display the questionnaire item by item following proper skip patterns, and record responses directly into machine-readable data files. This is a relatively new and still developing technology.

Controller of the sampling pool. The person responsible for releasing telephone numbers from the sampling pool and for making decisions about the final proper disposition of each number that has been released.

Conversion of refusals. The redialing of initial refusals one or more times in order to try to enhance the external validity of the final sample of completions by reducing the number of refusals.

Dialing disposition. The outcome of any dialing attempt of a telephone number released from a sampling pool. The disposition is typically recorded on the call-sheet following a numerical coding system.

Degree of precision. Also referred to as margin of error, this is the scientific measure of the precision of a survey based on its sampling error. The smaller the degree of precision, the more exact the estimates provided by the survey from the standpoint of sampling.

External validity. The accuracy with which one can generalize survey results from a sample to the population it purports to represent. This depends on many factors, including the sampling design and interviewing quality.

Fallback statements. Standardized responses for interviewers to provide when asked anticipated questions about the survey by a household gatekeeper or a respondent.

Fast-busy. A distinctly different repeating signal occasionally heard after a dialing. It is noticeably more rapid than a normal busy and often indicates that a number is not working or the dialing was not executed properly.

Gatekeeper. Anyone who an interviewer must "get past" in order to speak with a selected respondent. Typically the first person who answers the telephone when that person turns out not to be the selected respondent.

Hit rate. The proportion of telephone numbers in a sampling pool that lead to eligible respondents. In a general population survey the hit rate is typically the percentage of the sampling pool that reaches residences.

Household informant. Anyone in a household who can provide valid answers to an interviewer about the household. For example, anyone who can accurately report the number of persons living in the household as part of a respondent selection sequence.

Introduction/selection sheet. A separate sheet of paper attached to each call-sheet containing the introductory spiel and respondent selection technique employed in a survey.

Introductory spiel. The standardized introduction read by an interviewer when contact is made with a possible eligible household or respondent.

Margin of error. See *degree of precision.*

Pilot test. A relatively small number of practice interviews to test and further refine the wording of the introduction, selection procedure, and question-naire. Pilot tests also help determine how long it takes to administer the questionnaire. Typically, a debriefing session is held after the pilot-test with those interviewers who participated in it.

Population parameter. A value that represents the level at which some variable exists in a population. Surveys are typically used to estimate these parameters.

Prefix. The first three digits in a local telephone number; also referred to as a local telephone exchange.

Quality control. The system used in a telephone survey to enhance the quality of sampling and interviewing. Telephone surveys afford a greater opportunity for quality control than other survey methods.

Random-digit dialing. Several techniques that form sampling pools by adding random digits to prefixes known to ring in the sampling area, thereby forming the telephone numbers that are printed on call-sheets.

Respondent exclusion criteria. Any factor that makes a person ineligible to be chosen as a respondent; for example, being too young or too old.

Respondent selection. The technique used by interviewers after an introductory spiel to choose properly from among potentially eligible respondents within a sampling unit.

Response rates. Several approaches to calculating numerical measures of the efficiency of a sampling pool in reaching eligible respondents and the efficiency of interviewers in completing interviews with those eligible.

Reverse directory. A special telephone directory that has numbers ordered numerically and/or by street address, rather than alphabetically by last names. Unlisted telephone numbers will not appear in a reverse directory.

Role-playing. An interviewer training technique in which interviewers practice using a survey's introduction, selection procedure, and questionnaire with supervisory personnel acting the part of the respondent.

Sampling boundaries. The geographical area within which a telephone survey will sample respondents.

Sampling design. The overall manner in which a survey sample is chosen to represent some population of interest. It includes a decision of sampling boundaries, how the sampling pool will be formed, and how respondents will be chosen within a sampling unit.

Sampling pool. The set of telephone numbers that will be used by interviewers to reach respondents. Every number used from a sampling pool is printed on a separate call-sheet to control its proper processing.

Saturation. As applied to general population telephone surveys, the proportion of households in a sampling area with at least one telephone access line. In 1986, the saturation of telephones in U.S. residences was very likely in excess of 95%.

Skip pattern. Any sequence of items within a questionnaire that is contingent upon one or more previous answers.

Stratification by prefix. A sampling pool in which telephone numbers are proportionally represented in accordance with the actual prevalence of their prefix within the survey's sampling boundaries.

Suffix. The last four digits of a telephone number.

Systematic sampling. Different techniques that can be used to form sampling pools directly from telephone directories or other listings.

Unlisted telephone number. Any telephone number that is not published in a local telephone directory and will not be given out by a directory assistance operator.

Unpublished telephone number. Any telephone number that is not published in a local telephone directory. It may or may not be given out by directory assistance depending on local telephone company procedures.

Vacuous suffix bank. A range of telephone suffixes that contains no working telephone numbers.

Validation. The immediate review of a completed questionnaire by the supervisory personnel on duty at an interviewing session to determine that the interviewer properly completed the entire questionnaire and recorded open-ended responses legibly.

Verification. Calling a respondent backing to verify that an interview was in fact completed. Verification is done by supervisory personnel typically within a day or two after the completion.

Weighting. A post hoc statistical adjustment that is often used with survey data to enhance the external validity, and thus the accuracy, of the survey's estimates of population parameters.

REFERENCES

AT&T (1982). *The world's telephones: 1982.* Atlanta: R. H. Donnelley.

Babbie, E. (1973). *Survey research methods.* Belmont, CA: Wadsworth.

Babbie, E. (1983). *The practice of social research.* Belmont, CA: Wadsworth.

Belson, W. A. (1981). *The design and understanding of survey questions.* Aldershot, England: Gower Publications.

Bradburn, N. M., & Sudman, S. (1979). *Improving interview method and questionnaire design.* San Francisco: Jossey-Bass.

Brooks, J. (1976). *Telephone: The first hundred years.* New York: Harper & Row.

Bryant, B. E. (1975). Respondent selection in a time of changing household composition. *Journal of Marketing Research, 12,* 129-135.

Campbell, D. T., & Stanley, J. (1966). *Experimental and quasi-experimental designs for research.* Chicago: Rand-McNally.

Cochran, W. G. (1977). *Sampling techniques.* New York: John Wiley.

Cohen, J., & Cohen, P. (1983). *Applied multiple regression/correlation analysis for the behavioral sciences* (2nd ed.). Hillsdale, NJ: Lawrence Erlbaum.

Cook, T. D., & Campbell, D. T. (1979). *Quasi-experimentation: Designs and analysis issues for field settings* Boston: Houghton-Miflin.

Crano, W. D., & Brewer, M. B. (1973). *Principles of research in social psychology.* New York: McGraw-Hill.

Czaja, R., Blair, J., & Sebestik, J. (1982). Respondent selection in a telephone survey. *Journal of Marketing Research, 19,* 381-385.

Dawes, R. M. (1972). *Fundamentals of attitude measurment.* New York: John Wiley.

de Sola Pool, I. (1977). *The social impact of the telephone.* Cambridge: MIT Press.

Dillman, D. A. (1978). *Mail and telephone surveys: The total design method.* New York: John Wiley.

Dillman, D. A., Gallegos, J., & Frey, J. H. (1976). Reducing refusals for telephone interviews. *Public Opinion Quarterly, 40,* 99-114.

Edwards, J. (in press). *Self-report measures of knowledge, attitudes and behaviors.* Newbury Park, CA: Sage.

Ekman, P., & Friesen, W. (1974). Detecting deception from the body and face. *Journal of Personality and Social Psychology, 29,* 288-298.

Ekman, P., & Friesen, W. (1976). Body movement and voice pitch in deceptive interaction. *Semiotica, 16,* 23-27.

Fowler, F. J., Jr. (1984). *Survey research methods.* Beverly Hills, CA: Sage.

Frey, J. H. (1983). *Survey research by telephone.* Beverly Hills, CA: Sage.

Groves, R., & Kahn, M. (1979). *Surveys by telephone: A national comparison with personal interviews.* New York: Academic Press.

Hagen, D. E., & Collier, C. M. (1983). Must respondent selection procedures for telephone surveys be invasive? *Public Opinion Quarterly, 47,* 547-556.

Hays, W. L. (1973). *Statistics for the social sciences.* New York: Holt, Rinehart & Winston.

Henry, G. (in press). *Practical sampling.* Newbury Park, CA: Sage.

Kish, L. (1949). A procedure for objective respondent selection within the household. *Journal of the American Statistical Association, 44,* 380-387.

Kish, L. (1965). *Survey sampling.* New York: John Wiley .

Landon, E. L., & Banks, S. K. (1977). Relative efficiency and bias of plus-one telephone sampling. *Journal of Marketing Research, 14,* 294-299.

Lavrakas, P. J., & Maier, R. A. (1979). Differences in human ability to judge veracity from the audio medium. *Journal of Research in Personality, 13,* 139-153.

Lavrakas, P. J., & Maier, R. A., Jr. (1984). The magnitude and nature of RDD panel attrition. Evanston: Northwestern University Survey Laboratory. (mimeo)

Lavrakas, P. J., Skogan, W. G., Normoyle, J., Herz, E. J., Salem, G., & Lewis, D. A. (1980). *Factors related to citizen particpation in personal, household, and neighborhood anti-crime measures.* Evanston, IL: Center for Urban Affairs and Policy Research.

Lavrakas, P. J., & Tyler, T. R. (1983). *Low cost telephone surveys.* Paper presented at Evaluation '83, Chicago.

LeBaily, R., & Lavrakas, P. J. (1981). *Generating a random digit dialing sample for telephone surveys.* Paper at Issue '81, The Annual SPSS Convention, San Francisco.

Maier, N. R. F. (1966). Sensitivity to attempts at deception in an interview situation. *Personnel Psychology, 19,* 55-66.

Maier, N. R. F., & Thurber, J. (1968). Accuracy of judgments of deception when an interview is watched, heard or read. *Personnel Psychology, 21,* 23-30.

Maier, R. A., & Lavrakas, P. J. (1976). Lying behavior and evaluation of lies. *Perceptual and Motor Skills, 42,* 575-581.

Oldendick, R. W., Sorenson, S. B., Tuchfarber, A. J., & Bishop, G. F. (1985). *Last birthday respondent selection in telephone surveys: A further test.* Paper presented at the Midwest Association of Public Opinion Research meetings, Chicago.

O'Rourke, D., & Blair, J. (1983). Improving random respondent selection in telephone surveys. *Journal of Marketing Research, 20,* 428-432.

Pierce, J. R. (1977). The telephone and society in the past 100 years. In I. de Sola Pool (ed.), *The social impact of the telephone* (pp. 159-195). Cambridge: MIT Press.

Robinson, J. P., & Shaver, P. R. (1973). *Measurement of social psychological attitudes.* Ann Arbor: Institute for Social Research, University of Michigan.

Salmon, C. T., & Nichols, J. S. (1983). The next-birthday method for respondent selection. *Public Opinion Quarterly, 47,* 270-276.

Schuman, H., & Presser, S. (1981). *Questions and answers in attitude surveys.* New York: Academic Press.

Skogan, W. G. (1978). *The Center for Urban Affairs random digit dial telephone survey.* Evanston, IL: Center for Urban Affairs and Policy Research.

Sudman, S. (1973). The uses of telephone directories for survey sampling. *Journal of Marketing Research, 10,* 204-207.

Sudman, S., (1976). *Applied sampling.* New York: Academic Press.

Sudman, S., & Bradburn, N. (1974). *Response effects in surveys: a review and synthesis.* Chicago: Aldine.

Sudman, S. & Bradburn, N. (1982). *Asking questions.* San Francisco: Jossey-Bass.

Troldahl, V. C., & Carter, R. E., Jr. (1964). Random selection of respondents within households in phone surveys. *Journal of Marketing Research, 1,* 71-76.

U.S. Bureau of the Census. (1984). *Statistical abstracts of the United States, 1984.* Washington, DC: U.S. Government Printing Office.

Waksberg, J. (1978). Sampling methods for random digit dialing. *Journal of the American Statistical Association, 73,* 40-46.

Weiss, C. (1972). *Evaluation research.* Englewood Cliffs, NJ: Prentice-Hall.

INDEX

ABOUT THE AUTHOR

Paul J. Lavrakas is Associate Professor at Northwestern University's Medill School of Journalism and Director of the Northwestern University Survey Laboratory. He received a B.A. (1968) in general social sciences from Michigan State University, an M.A. (1975) in experimental social psychology from Loyola University of Chicago, and a Ph.D. (1977) in applied social psychology from Loyola. From 1968 through 1972, he taught fifth grade in a public school on Chicago's southside. He served as a public sector specialist for the Westinghouse Electric Corporation in 1977 before becoming a Research Associate of Northwestern University's Center for Urban Affairs and Policy Research in 1978. During the past twelve years he has gained an international reputation for his extensive research, evaluations, and policy writings in the area of citizens' reactions to crime and community crime prevention. Related to this, he is active as a consultant for the National Institute of Justice, the Office of Juvenile Justice and Delinquency Prevention, and the National Crime Prevention Coalition. For the past few years Dr. Lavrakas has focused on methodological research for improving survey techniques, especially those used in gathering information on newspaper readership and related attitudes.

NOTES